≠23097002

ECE/EB.AIR/25

KV-038-740

ECONOMIC COMMISSION FOR EUROPE
Geneva

Air Pollution Studies 6

THE STATE
OF TRANSBOUNDARY
AIR POLLUTION:
1989 UPDATE

*Report prepared within the framework of
the Convention on
Long-range Transboundary Air Pollution*

D

624 53
STA

UNITED NATIONS
New York, 1990

NOTE

Symbols of United Nations documents are composed of capital letters combined with figures. Mention of such a symbol indicates a reference to a United Nations document.

* * *

The designations employed and the presentation of the material in this publication do not imply the expression of any opinion whatsoever on the part of the Secretariat of the United Nations concerning the legal status of any country, territory, city or area or of its authorities, or concerning the delimitation of its frontiers or boundaries.

ECE/EB.AIR/25

UNITED NATIONS PUBLICATION

Sales No. E.90.II.E.33

ISBN 92-1-116489-3
ISSN 1014-4625

02500P

Contents

INTRODUCTION AND SUMMARY

This sixth volume of the series of *Air Pollution Studies* published under the auspices of the Executive Body for the **Convention on Long-range Transboundary Air Pollution**, contains the documents reviewed and approved for publication at the seventh session of the Executive Body held at Geneva from 21 to 24 November 1989.

Part one is the **annual review of strategies and policies** for air pollution abatement. It updates the previous annual review published in 1989 (*The state of Transboundary Air Pollution, Air Pollution Studies No.5*, Sales No. E.89.II.E.25), on the basis of national data and reports reviewed up to 31 December 1989. The focus of the review is on policy measures to implement the 1979 Convention and its related protocols on sulphur compounds (Helsinki, 1985) and nitrogen oxides (Sofia, 1988). Country by country, recent legislative and regulatory developments are summarized, including ambient-air quality standards, fuel-quality standards, emission standards, as well as economic instruments for air pollution abatement. Information is provided on control technologies required and in operation in Europe and North America for stationary and mobile emission sources, and on existing administrative structures for air quality management, monitoring, assessment and research. Besides ongoing activities under the Convention, the review also covers other multilateral and bilateral arrangements in the ECE region, and related global concerns. The tables give national emission data and forecasts for sulphur dioxide (SO_2), nitrogen oxides (NO_x) and volatile organic compounds (VOCs), from 1980 to 2005.

Part two is an executive summary of the 1988 forest damage survey in Europe, carried out under the **International Co-operative Programme for Assessment and Monitoring of Air Pollution Effects on Forests** which was established by the Executive Body for the Convention in 1985. This was the third annual survey undertaken by the programme; the full report has been published as part of a joint project by ECE and the United Nations Environment Programme (*Forest Damage and Air Pollution: Report of the 1988 Forest Damage Survey in Europe*, FP/9101-86-05, 1988, 87pp.). A total of 25 countries participated in the survey, conducted in accordance with common guidelines laid down in an ECE manual on methodologies and criteria for harmonized sampling, assessment, monitoring and analysis of the effects of air pollution on forests. Tables show the geographical coverage of the survey and the degree of defoliation reported by countries for different coniferous and broadleaved species, with a comparison of the 1986, 1987 and 1988 survey results.

Parts three and four describe the **effects of mercury and some other heavy metals related to the long-range atmospheric transport** of pollution. These sections were prepared by rapporteurs from the Swedish National Environmental Protection Board and the Swedish Institute of Water and Air Research. The section on mercury describes the environmental effects and the causes of mercury pollution in air and atmospheric deposition, including its sources and its transport from forest soils into fresh water and aquatic organisms. The section dealing with other heavy metals (such as asbestos, cadmium and lead) describes the process of atmospheric transport and deposition, the effects on forest ecosystems, ground water, surface water and agricultural products.

Part five analyses the **economic and cost impact of different strategies for abatement** of sulphur oxides (SO_x) and nitrogen oxides (NO_x) emissions. Macro-economic impacts include effects on gross domestic product/net material product, employment, prices, energy demand, industrial structure and international trade/competitiveness. Specific examples of cost impact are provided from eight countries in Eastern and Western Europe, including detailed information on investments and operational costs for air pollution reductions.

Apart from necessary editing, care has been taken to avoid any substantive change in the documents as reviewed by the Executive Body for the Convention.[1] Sole responsibility for the text rests with the secretariat of the United Nations Economic Commission for Europe.

---

1 Part one appeared as a document under the symbol EB.AIR/R.40; part two as EB.AIR/WG.1/R.35/Rev.1; part three as EB.AIR/WG.1/R.36; part four as EB.AIR/WG.1/R.37; part five as EB.AIR/GE.2/R.18 and Addendum 1.

Part ONE

ANNUAL REVIEW OF STRATEGIES AND POLICIES FOR AIR POLLUTION ABATEMENT

According to the work plan for implementation of the Convention on Long-range Transboundary Air Pollution (ECE/EB.AIR/20, annex IV, item 1.1.1), Parties and Signatories submit information annually on recent developments in national strategies and policies with regard to the initiation or implementation of reductions of relevant emissions. The information includes, in particular, actual levels of emissions of sulphur compounds, nitrogen oxides and other agreed pollutants. According to the guidelines for reporting by Parties to the 1985 Helsinki Protocol, as adopted by the Executive Body at its fifth session (ECE/EB.AIR/16, annex IV, paragraph 3), Parties must also report no later than 1 May of each year on national programmes, policies and strategies for sulphur emission reductions and on progress towards achieving the goal of the Protocol, i.e. the reduction of sulphur emissions or their transboundary fluxes by at least 30 per cent. Furthermore, in accordance with article 8 of the 1988 Sofia Protocol, as adopted at the sixth session of the Executive Body (ECE/EB.AIR/18, annex I), Parties exchange information on national programmes, policies and strategies that shall serve as a means of controlling and reducing emissions of nitrogen oxides or their transboundary fluxes.

The present review is based on information provided in national submissions and other official sources of information received up to 31 December 1989. Country-by-country emission data and forecasts for the years 1980 to 2005 are given in tables 1 to 3. They reflect all corrections and new information received from Parties as of 1 September 1990 regarding total national emissions of sulphur dioxide (SO_2), nitrogen oxides (NO_x) and non-methane hydrocarbons/volatile organic compounds (VOCs).

Chapter 1: NATIONAL STRATEGIES

Several Parties have reported on the preparation and implementation of comprehensive programmes for air pollution abatement.

Belgium gives priority to measures against air pollution from large combustion sources and from motor vehicles.

In accordance with its long-term strategy and policy **Bulgaria** is taking further steps to implement the Convention on Long-range Transboundary Air Pollution (Geneva, 1979) and its Protocols (Helsinki, 1985; Sofia, 1988). In the chemical industry for example, two lines for the production of sulphuric acid have been stopped at one large chemical plant. As a result, annual emissions of SO_2 have been reduced by 10,000 tons.

In **Canada**, the Federal Government and seven Eastern provincial governments have formalized agreements to reduce SO_2 emissions in the region to 2.3 million tonnes by 1994, a reduction of 50 per cent of 1980 allowable levels. The reduction is absolute, requiring major reductions at existing sources as well as control of emissions from new sources. As a result of the control programme, SO_2 emissions in eastern Canada have now been reduced by nearly 40 per cent of their 1980 base levels. Ground level ozone is the key NO_x- and VOC-related air pollution problem in Canada. Canada currently has in place stringent vehicle emission standards, including the use of three-way catalytic converters on passenger vehicles that will maintain NO_x emissions at their current levels until the mid-1990s. In addition, all 11 Federal and Provincial Environment Ministers have directed officials to develop, by the summer of 1990, a national plan of action to further manage NO_x and VOC emissions. The plan of action will prevent increased emissions of NO_x and VOCs beyond 1995. In formulating its NO_x and VOC management plan, Canada will also incorporate energy efficiency, conservation and the use of alternative fuels in addition to the traditional regulatory approach.

A new energy plan and a traffic action plan is being prepared in **Denmark** to follow up the Government's Action Plan on Environment and Development. Both plans are based on the Brundtland Commission report on sustainable development. The objective is to point out specific options for the reduction of the pollution load from the energy and traffic sectors. The plans are to be presented to the Danish Parliament in spring 1990.

In **Finland**, the Ministry of Environment has established two working groups to investigate how nitrogen oxide emissions can be reduced. The first group investigates and recommends reductions of nitrogen oxide emissions from new and existing boilers. The second group investigates and recommends reductions of nitrogen emissions from motor vehicles, by changes in the transportation infrastructure and other means. Both groups are expected to finalize their work in 1989. The 45 per cent reduction of the 1980 level for sulphur emissions is mainly due to structural changes such as the introduction of nuclear power, switching from heavy fuel oil to hard coal, and development of processes in the pulp and paper industry and chemical industries. Work has started on further reductions of sulphur emissions, the target being a reduction of about 70 to 80 per cent of 1980 emissions.

In **France**, the main objective of air pollution prevention strategies has been the improvement of air quality in the most polluted (industrial and urban) areas. Present strategies focus on the reduction of acidifying pollutants and photooxidants to the maximum extent possible without excessive costs, taking into account the most recent technological developments. High priority is given to measures for the reduction of hydrocarbons and nitrogen oxides. France intends to reduce SO_2 emissions by at least 50 per cent between 1980 and 1990; hydrocarbon emissions by 30 per cent between 1985 and 2000; and NO_x emissions by 30 per cent between 1980 and 1998.

In the **Federal Republic of Germany**, strategies for air pollution abatement are the main focus of the fourth parliamentary report on environmental policy, submitted by the Federal Ministry of Environment, Nature Protection and Reactor Safety in July 1988. The report emphasizes the principle of preventive action (*Vorsorgeprinzip*), the polluter-pays principle, and the principle of co-operation to ensure the adaptation of economic decision-making to ecological requirements, es-

pecially in the field of energy use. Emission reduction targets for the period up to 1995 are specified for SO_2, NO_x, CO, particulates and VOCs.

In **Hungary**, the Council of Ministers in April 1989 decided on a series of policy measures to implement the 1988 Sofia Protocol on Nitrogen Oxides, including the future introduction of three-way catalytic converters for motor vehicles; low-NO_x burners and other modifications for utility boilers; and various incentives to promote energy saving and rail transport.

In the **Netherlands**, a National Environmental Policy Plan (NEPP) was submitted to Parliament in May 1989. The plan proposes a medium-term strategy for policy actions to be taken during the period from 1990 to 1994, and long-term objectives up to the year 2010, with a view to achieving sustainable development. An Acidification Abatement Plan, implementing the policy concerning acidification as set out in the NEPP, was submitted to Parliament in July 1989. It includes specific objectives for the reduction of acid deposition. A target load of 1,400 equivalents per ha/y has to be reached in 2010. Interim target loads are 2,400 acid equivalents in 2,000 and 4,000 acid equivalents per ha/y in 1994. Total emissions of SO_2, NO_x, NH_3 and VOCs will be reduced in 2000 by 80 per cent, 50 per cent, 70 per cent and 60 per cent respectively, relative to 1980 levels.

In **Norway**, a programme for NO_x reduction was approved by Parliament in June 1988. The NO_x programme includes further measures concerning motor vehicles, emission controls for sea transport and more stringent controls for stationary sources. A more detailed programme for NO_x reductions to implement the 1988 Sofia Protocol is under preparation. A programme for the further reduction of SO_2 emissions (by 50 per cent of the 1980 level by 1993, and subsequently down to critical loads) has been prepared. The programme includes stringent demands on process industry, on sulphur contents in light and heavy fuel oil, and proposals for energy saving.

In **Sweden**, the long-term goal adopted by Parliament in 1988 is to reduce SO_2 emissions by 80 per cent between 1980 and 2000, with possible options to achieve this goal to be presented in a new action programme against air pollution and acidification in 1990. In relation to nitrogen oxides, efforts will be undertaken to decrease NO_x emissions by 30 per cent between 1980 and 1995. Possibilities of reducing total Swedish emissions of NO_x by 50 per cent between 1980 and 2000 will be explored in the action programme to be presented in 1990. Anthropogenic emissions of hydrocarbons in Sweden are expected to fall by some 25 per cent between 1980 and 1995 as a result of existing environmental standards and decisions already taken. The lower emissions predicted will be primarily due to more stringent hydrocarbon emission standards for cars, including standards for evaporative emissions. A special programme for reducing emissions of hydrocarbons is under preparation.

In **Switzerland**, the Federal Council has confirmed a series of policy decisions for air pollution abatement, in the light of the recommendations of an expert study commissioned to determine ways and means to meet the agreed reduction targets for 1995, i.e. to reach the 1960 level of emissions of SO_2, NO_x and VOCs. The policy options identified for this purpose include economic incentive charges on fossil fuels and VOC uses; an emission-related tax on heavy-duty vehicles; and a mileage-related ecological bonus for passenger cars and light-duty vehicles.

In **Turkey**, one of the environment sector *ad hoc* expert committees formed simultaneously with the start of the preliminary work for the 6th Five Year Development Plant is the *Ad Hoc* Air Quality Management Experts Committee. The Committee carries out activities on identification of factors affecting air quality in all provinces; emission inventories; determination of air quality; determination of control technologies; preparation of amendments to the Air Quality Control Regulations; supporting research on air quality; and development of control technolgies.

In the **Union of Soviet Socialist Republics**, a draft *Long-term State Programme for Environmental Conservation and the Rational Exploitation of the Natural Resources for the 13th Five-Year Plan and in Prospect up to the Year 2005* was prepared in 1989. Its general purpose is to guarantee favourable conditions for the health of the present and future generations, the conservation of the biosphere and the reproduction of natural-resource potential in the interests of efficient and reliable socio-economic development. The programme envisages that health and hygiene standards for the quality of the atmosphere in urban and industrial centres of the USSR will be achieved in stages by 2005. For this purpose it is proposed to reduce, by comparison with 1986, industrial discharges into the atmosphere by the year 1995 by a factor of 1.3, and by 2005 by a factor of 2.0, including solid substances by 2.4, sulphur dioxide by more than 2, nitrogen oxides by 1.5, carbon monoxide by 1.8, hydrocarbons by 1.7, and also to reduce by approximately 80 per cent the emissions of specific pollutants at enterprises situated in 276 towns where there is excess content of these substances in the atmos-

phere. Sulphur compound emissions in the European territory of the USSR shall be reduced by 30 per cent by 1993 and by 60 per cent by 2005; and nitrogen oxide emissions shall be stabilized at their 1987 level by 1994.

In **Yugoslavia**, work has started on the formulation of an Environmental Protection Strategy which will include a specific Air Pollution Prevention Strategy.

Chapter 2: NATIONAL POLICY MEASURES

I. Legislation and regulatory provisions

Changes in legislation and regulatory provisions have been reported by several countries.

In **Austria**, two constitutional amendments were adopted in 1989 which relate to air pollution: the federal Government was entrusted with full regulatory powers in the field of air pollution control with the exception of domestic heating, which continues to be regulated by regional (state) authorities. Under a 1988 amendment of the Industrial Code, all new plants must reduce emissions in accordance with best available technology, while existing plants may have to take additional control measures in case of significant environmental harm. A new Clean Air Act for Steam Boilers entered into force in January 1989, with tightened emission standards and a duty of monthly emission reports. The new Emergency Air Pollution Control Act allows for the declaration of a region as heavily polluted if certain concentration levels of air pollutants are exceeded (smog alert), in which case emergency control plans become applicable.

In **Denmark**, a new law for the reduction of SO_2 and NO_x from power plants was adopted by Parliament in March 1989, replacing the 1984 law for the reduction of SO_2 from power plants.

In **Finland**, the Ministry of Transport amended the Motor Vehicles Decree and its Road Traffic Decisions in October 1988, in implementation of the Council of State's decisions on air pollution abatement.

In **Italy**, a guideline to establish criteria and schedule dates for emission reductions is about to be issued. This Prime Minister's decree will contain nationwide emission limit values for the main industrial pollutants, including carcinogenic substances, heavy metals, toxic gases and VOCs. Existing plants must respect these limits within a number of years ranging from two to eight, according to their emission quality and quantity.

In **Portugal**, a new Air Quality Framework Act (*Lei Quadro do Ar*) is in preparation. New regulations for the establishment and operation of industrial plants are also expected to enter into force before the end of 1989.

In the **Union of Soviet Socialist Republics**, preparations for a new draft law on nature conservation will be completed in 1989, including provisions relevant to air quality control.

In the **United Kingdom**, the introduction of legislation to establish integrated pollution control will involve specifying some additional polluting processes for control by the central pollution inspectorates. Best Available Technology Not Entailing Excessive Costs (BATNEEC) will be required to minimize polluting emissions at source and to ensure that no environmental harm is caused. The Government of the United Kingdom also plans to include in this legislation, measures enabling it to implement the provisions of the EEC Large Combustion Plant Directive and provide for more public access to information about industrial pollution.

In the **United States of America**, the Federal Government proposed major amendments to the 1970 Clean Air Act in July 1989 which, if adopted by Congress, will also have important consequences for the reduction of transboundary air pollution. The proposal aims at halving SO_2 emissions from power stations by the end of the century, and to reduce toxic and carcinogenic air pollutants by three quarters over the same period. VOC emissions are to be reduced by 40 per cent by the year 2005, mainly by more stringent motor vehicle standards and by promoting the use of alternative fuels such as methanol.

In **Yugoslavia**, a Federal Air Pollution Prevention Act is in the process of being adopted in the Federal Assembly.

In 1989, the **European Economic Community** amended Regulation 3528/86 on the protection of the Community's forests against atmospheric pollution. Council Directives 89/369/EEC and 89/429/EEC on air pollution from new and existing municipal waste incineration plants were adopted in June 1989, defining emission limit values for total dust, heavy metals, hydrochloric acid, hydrofluoric acid and sulphur dioxide. The Directives also limit concentrations of carbon monoxide and organic compounds and specify measurements to be taken.

A. Ambient air quality standards

In **Austria**, the Emergency Air Pollution Control Act defines alert levels and emergency levels for SO_2, particulates, NO_2 and CO. New ambient air quality standards concerning these pollutants will be in force as of 1 January 1990. **Belgium** has implemented air quality standards for SO_2, particulates and NO_2 in accordance with EEC directives. In **Denmark**, the National Environmental Protection Agency launched on 1 January 1989 a three-year pilot project for the establishment of early warning of high pollution levels (smog emergency). In **Norway**, national guideline values related to health effects have been established for SO_2, total suspended particulates, NO_2, CO, photochemical oxidants and fluorides. **Portugal** incorporated into national law, by a regulation in March 1987, the EEC directives on SO_2, particulates, NO_2 and lead. Limit values and guideline values for O_3 and CO are contained in the new Air Quality Framework Act. **Turkey** has ambient air quality standards for SO_2, NO_x and particulates. The **United Kingdom** introduced regulations formalizing current practice to set air quality standards for SO_2, suspended particulate matter, lead and NO_x. In June 1989, the **European Economic Community** amended Council Directive 80/779/EEC on air quality limit values and guideline values for SO_2 and suspended particulates.

B. Fuel quality standards

In **Austria**, the 1988 Ordinance on Limiting the Sulphur Content of Fuel Oil limits the sulphur content of extra-light fuel oil to 0.2 per cent, of light fuel oil to 0.3 per cent, and medium fuel oil to 0.6 per cent. Heavy fuel oil is limited to a sulphur content of 2 per cent, with a further restriction to 1 per cent after 1 January 1992.

In **Canada**, the Federal Ministry of the Environment now envisages a phase-out of all leaded petrol by 31 December 1990.

In **Denmark**, the existing limits for sulphur content in fuel have become stricter from November 1988 onwards. The limit is now 1 per cent for heavy fuel oil, 0.2 per cent for gas oil and 0.9 per cent for coal and other fuels. The sale of lead-free petrol was further favoured by tax-reductions, the tax differentiation being raised from 0,47 to 0.57 DKr per litre of petrol. In April 1989 the share of lead-free petrol sales was about 37 per cent. This share was expected to rise substantially with the introduction of a lead-free premium in June 1989.

In order to achieve the goal to provide reasonably priced lead-free fuel all over the country,

Finland prohibited the production and import of leaded petrol (octane value 92) from September 1989. Lead-free 95-octane petrol is available at almost all 2,000 filling stations. The market share of unleaded petrol in the form of lead-free and mixed qualities is 40 per cent.

In **France**, a ministerial regulation of 9 June 1989 limits lead content in petrol to 0,25 g/l from August 1989 and to 0.15 g/l as from June 1991.

In the **Federal Republic of Germany**, since March 1988, a maximum sulphur content of 0.2 per cent may not be exceeded for light heating oil and diesel fuel. An extensive amendment to the Ordinance on Combustion Plants will lead to a further significant reduction in pollutant emissions from private households and other small combustion installations.

In **Ireland**, the 1989 Regulations on the Sulphur Content of Gas Oil prohibit the marketing of gas oil with a sulphur content exceeding 0.3 per cent in weight.

In **Italy**, lead-free petrol has been available in the whole national territory since April 1989.

In **Luxembourg**, the sulphur content of heavy fuel oil is limited to 1 per cent, and of gas oil to 0.2 per cent. Lead content of petrol is limited to 0.15 g/l; regular leaded petrol is forbidden.

In **Portugal**, a regulation of February 1989 limits sulphur content to 0.3 per cent for gas oil, 1 per cent for diesel oil, 2 per cent for heating oil, 3 per cent for light fuel oil and 3.5 per cent for heavy f uel oil.

In **Sweden**, as from January 1989, sulphur emissions from combustion (all fuels) must not exceed 0.19 mg sulphur/megajoule fuel input (corresponding to 0.8 per cent of sulphur in heavy fuel oil).

In **Switzerland**, the Federal Council decided in February 1989 to reduce the sulphur content of extra-light fuel oil from 0.2 per cent to 0.1 per cent, by way of taxation measures.

In **Turkey**, oil refineries carried out the necessary technical modifications in 1988 to reduce the lead content of petrol to 0.15 g/l. Production of petrol at this quality level has started. Lignites which are the main fuel source are also one of the main sources of air pollution. Priority has been given to raise the quality level of fuels used in big cities. By the use of imported coal, improvements in air quality were obtained. Studies have been concluded concerning the utilization of natural gas to be imported from the USSR. The Municipality of Greater Ankara is continuing the installation of main pipes for natural gas to be used for heating purposes. Fuel quality standards are in force for diesel oil (CO, NO_x, SO_2 and particulates) and for gaseous fuel (SO_2 and particulates).

In the **Union of Soviet Socialist Republics**, sulphur content in fuel is regulated by a State standard which at present is 2 per cent for light fuel oil, 3.5 per cent for medium oil and above 3.5 per cent for heavy fuel oil. In industrial centres with high air pollution levels, a general limit of 2 per cent is applied. New standards with more stringent requirements are currently in preparation.

The **United Kingdom** promoted the use of unleaded petrol by introducing the second largest tax differential in the European Community between leaded and unleaded fuel. Unleaded petrol now accounts for over 25 per cent of the market compared with an average of 1 per cent for 1988 and is now available in over 80 per cent of retail outlets.

C. Emission standards

In **Austria**, more stringent emission standards for new and existing steam boilers have been in force since 1 January 1989. Existing plants will have to comply with the new standards within the next six years. The new Clean Air Act for Steam Boilers also covers a variety of other pollutants with regard to municipal waste incineration. The sulphur content of fuels used in small steam boilers (3-10 MW$_{th}$) may not exceed 0.6 per cent for fuel oil, and for coal-fired plants smaller than 10 MW$_{th}$ it will be limited to 1 per cent, from 1 January 1992.

In **Belgium**, a Royal Decree modifying current standards for pollutant emissions from existing large combustion plants is under preparation.

In **Canada**, the Federal Government is setting up, over a five-year period, regulations to control emissions from internal combustion engines and their fuels. As a component of this plan, Federal Ministers of Environment and Transport were expected to give formal notice in December 1989 of their intent to issue a regulation aimed at the proposed California standards for hydrocarbons (0,25 grams/mile) carbon monoxide (0,4 grams/mile) and nitrogen oxides (0.4 grams/mile). This new regulation will be effective for 1994 model-year cars.

Denmark expects an increase in the use of natural gas for the generation of electricity. The Minister for the Environment has therefore found it necessary to regulate also the emission of nitrogen oxides from gas engine and turbines. A statutory order is being prepared covering all gas engines and turbines except a few installations covered by the special Act on SO_2 and NO_x. The statutory order is expected to enter into force at the beginning of 1990.

France is enforcing compliance with existing emission standards for hydrocarbons, in order to stop increasing emissions as a first step, and to reduce hydrocarbon emissions by 30 per cent by the year 2000. In particular, following earlier agreements with specific industrial sectors, technical instructions for the printing industry and the coil-coating industry were issued in 1988.

Emission limits in **Ireland** are based on European Community Directive 88/609/EEC requiring that emissions of sulphur dioxide and nitrogen oxides from large combustion plants be contained below given levels. In the case of existing plants, by 1993 SO_2 emissions must not exceed 124,000 tonnes with no increases between then and 2003, while by 1993 NO_x emissions must not exceed 50,000 tonnes by 1993 with no increase in the period up to 1998. In addition, emission limit values for SO_2, NO_x and smoke, which vary according to plant site, must be imposed on all new plants.

In **Italy**, European Community Directive 88/609/EEC on the limitation of emissions from large combustions plants with a thermal capacity equal to or larger than 50 MW, was adopted by a ministerial decree in May 1989. Emission limit values for SO_2, NO_x and dust are fixed in compliance with the Directive. More stringent limits are fixed for NO_x emissions from plants larger than 500 MW (200 mg/Nm3) and for dust when solid fuel is used (50 mg/Nm3). Limits for exhaust emissions from motor vehicles as contained in the Luxembourg agreement have been introduced by ministerial decree and will come into force according to the timetable set in the European Community Directives.

In **Norway**, new hydrocarbon emission standards for petrol-powered passenger cars (0.25 g/km exhaust, 2 g/test evaporation) became effective in January 1989, and will gradually be introduced for diesel cars (0.25 g/km from January 1990), light-duty trucks (0.5 g/km by the end of 1991) and heavy-duty trucks (1.2g/kWh by the end of 1993).

In **Sweden**, new emission limits for SO_2 will be introduced successively as from 1993, starting with the southernmost counties and the counties with the largest cities. The emission limits to be introduced in the 1990s are to be calculated as annual mean values. For a district heating system, the emission limit applies to the system as a whole; similarly, for several combustion units within an industrial plant, the emission limit applies to all of the units combined.

In **Portugal**, the draft Air Quality Framework Act scheduled to enter into force in 1989 contains detailed limit values for pollutant emissions from large combustion plants and for other industrial installations such as pulp and paper, construction material, the chemical industry, glass production, iron and steel, some food processing industries, and waste incineration.

In the **Ukrainian Soviet Socialist Republic**, standards of maximum permissible atmospheric emissions (MPE) have been laid down for enterprises whose emissions total over 97 per cent of the combined emissions in the Republic. By the beginning of 1991, MPE standards are expected to be established for all enterprises in the Republic which are situated within urban or industrial centres and which emit pollutants into the atmosphere.

On 24 November 1988, the **European Economic Community** adopted Council Directive 88/609/EEC on the limitation of emissions of certain pollutants into the air from large combustion plants. The Directive specifies ceilings and reduction targets for emissions of SO_2, NO_x and dust for new plants and existing plants, to be implemented by member countries by 30 June 1990.

D. Licensing of potentially polluting activities

In the **Federal Republic of Germany**, the general obligations of operators of facilities subject to licensing were extended to include rules on waste minimization and the use of waste heat. In **Ireland** the regulations of the licensing system for emissions from industrial plants provide for licensing for 30 industrial processes in the case of new plants and major alterations to existing plants and for 10 classes of existing plants. The classes of existing plants which are licensable may be extended by regulation under the Air Pollution Act. In **Italy**, according to a Prime Minister's decree all existing industrial installations in case of renewal of their licence are bound to declare the amount and composition of their emissions and to present before 30 July 1990 an operative project to reduce their emissions. **Luxembourg** has introduced a new licensing procedure for all combustion plants with a thermal capacity exceeding 3 MW. In **Portugal**, the new Air Quality Framework Act requires that specified new industrial projects or changes in existing ones will be subject to licensing by the General Directorate for Environmental Quality. In **Turkey**, an emission permit project was started in November 1986 and to date 1,100 establishments have obtained licences from the authorities after submitting information on emission measurements and documents concerning emission control facilities. As the procedure will take two to three years, existing establishments have been granted extra time for remedial action. The licensing procedure is expected to be completed for all establishments by 1991/1992. In the **Ukrainian Soviet Socialist Republic**, emission permits have been issued to enterprises whose combined emissions represent 95 per cent of the total emission capacity in the Republic.

E. *Physical planning and zoning*

In the **Byelorussian Soviet Socialist Republic**, air pollution control measures are included among the environmental factors to be taken into account in the physical planning of urban, industrial and natural zones. In **France**, special protection zones where SO_2 emissions are restricted have been established for Paris and its vicinity, Lyon-Villeurbanne, Marseille, and the Lille-Roubaix-Tourcoing area; a further special protection zone is planned for Strasbourg. In **Ireland** the Air Pollution Act provides for the establishment of special control areas to prevent or limit air pollution. Air quality standards for suspended particulates are being exceeded in certain parts of Dublin and a programme for special control area orders is in operation. Three orders have been confirmed for areas comprising 20,000 houses and other premises. These require that only smokeless or low smoke fuels be used. Further orders for areas covering over 20,000 houses and other premises are in preparation. A general policy directive was issued by the Minister for the Environment under the Planning Acts in December 1988 to planning authorities and the Planning Appeals Board requiring them, in considering development applications in built-up areas where smoke may be a problem, to take account of the need for combustion appliance and fuels to limit smoke emissions. In **Turkey**, the city of Ankara recorded a considerable reduction in air pollution, mainly by prohibiting the burning of lignite and of fuels with a sulphur content exceeding 1 per cent and a volatile organic matter content exceeding 10 per cent in the city area. In the **Union of Soviet Socialist Republics**, health protection zones are being established for industrial activities, on the basis of applicable public health standards.

F. *Other regulatory measures*

In order to control VOC emissions in the **Federal Republic of Germany**, regulations requiring anti-evaporation equipment at filling stations are now in preparation. In **Norway**, offset plants in the printing industry will be required to reduce their VOC emissions to 20-50 mg/m3 by the end of 1989; a similar emission limit is expected to be introduced for the package printing and plastic (PVC) coating industries. In **Portugal**, a decree on environmental impact assessment pursuant to the 1987 Basic Environment Act is currently in preparation. In **Switzerland**, the measures decided by the Federal Council in August 1989 include mandatory emission controls for light and heavy diesel vehicles, measures to reduce fuel evaporation losses, and various means to promote rail transport and combined freight transport. The **Union of Soviet Socialist Republics** emphasizes measures for the rational organization of urban motor vehicle traffic in the European part of the USSR.

II. Economic incentives and disincentives

A. *Subsidies*

In **Greece**, tax reductions between 250,000 and 1,500,000 drachmas are planned for "clean cars" adhering to strict emission standards. In the **Federal Republic of Germany**, new tax incentives will become effective in January 1990 for new and retrofitted low-pollution vehicles; these incentives will apply until 1991 when more stringent emission standards will become mandatory. Anticipating the entry into force of the relevant EEC Directive, tax incentives have been in force in the Netherlands since March 1989 for new petrol or LPG-powered passenger cars which comply with US-83 or equivalent standards. In **Portugal**, a financial incentive system for economic adjustment to the EEC Common Market (SINPEDIP) allows support to industries for the acquisition of pollution control equipment, by subsidies equivalent to 50 per cent of the investment up to a maximum of 75 million Escudos per project. There are also tax allowances for anti-pollution investments, and an incentive system for rational energy utilization (SIURE). In **Sweden**, advance compliance with the new emission standards for buses and trucks (which will be compulsory from 1992 onwards for light-duty vehicles and from 1994 onwards for heavy-duty vehicles) is promoted by economic incentives during the two years before they become mandatory. A total of SEK 450 million has been allocated for this purpose. A subsidy of SEK 1,000 per vehicle is available for the installation of equipment reducing emissions by at least 40 per cent. **Switzerland** plans to introduce differentiated taxation and/or differentiated insurance contributions for low-pollution motor vehicles. In **Turkey**, up to 45 per cent of expenditures necessary for the prevention of environmental pollution and improvement of the environment shall be provided from the Environmental Protection Fund by credits with a maximum term of 20 years.

B. Fuel tax measures

In **France,** the tax on lead-free petrol has been reduced by 41 centimes as of 1 July 1989. Thus at the pump lead-free petrol will be approximately 10 centimes per litre cheaper than leaded petrol. In **Ireland,** the 1988 and 1989 national budgets provided tax adjustments which transformed a cost disadvantage of over 4 pence per gallon into an advantage of 5 pence per gallon for unleaded petrol. The national distribution network for unleaded petrol now consists of about 1,000 outlets or over 30 per cent of the total number of outlets. In **Italy** a financial law was issued in September 1989 reducing duty on lead-free petrol by 50 lire per litre. The Government of **Norway** has proposed to raise the tax on lead-free petrol by 3 per cent and the tax on leaded petrol by 4 per cent. The tax difference will thus increase from NOK 0.32 in 1988 to NOK 0.36 in 1989. In addition, the tax on sulphur in fuel oil will increase by 67 per cent between 1988 and 1989. In **Portugal,** lead-free petrol is available at a lower price than leaded petrol. In the **Union of Soviet Socialist Republics,** a system of discounts and surcharges on fuel prices according to sulphur content is currently being developed.

C. Emission charges and fines

In **Portugal,** the new Air Quality Framework Act foresees the creation of a prorated emission charge on air pollutants, with the proceeds allocated to anti-pollution programmes. **Sweden** has introduced a special emission charge for nitrogen oxide emissions from all domestic aircraft. The **Union of Soviet Socialist Republics** will introduce a system of emission charges for industrial establishments from 1991 onwards, which will start on an experimental basis in Moscow, Zaporozhe and the Donetsk District in 1989. Revenue from these charges, prorated according to the amount of air pollutants emitted, will be allocated to regional nature conservation funds.

D. Other economic instruments

Finland is using environmental taxes to influence emission levels. The Government has proposed for 1990, *inter alia*, carbon dioxide taxes, which are expected to raise the price of gas by 2 per cent and the price of coal by 8 per cent. Taxes for environmental investments and clean vehicles have been reduced.

III. Control technologies required and in operation

A. Stationary sources

In **Austria,** a 1988 amendment to the Industrial Code stipulates that all new plants are obliged to reduce their emissions according to the best available technology. Existing plants have to implement additional emission control measures, if measurements or complaints in the immediate neighbourhood show that the emissions result in significant harm to the environment.

In **Bulgaria,** the Government has approved the construction of sulphur-emission control technologies at 12 large coal-fired power stations. It has also earmarked 14 thermal power stations for the introduction of new burners, reducing NO_x in the combustion chamber by 10-15 per cent. In addition, a large catalytic reduction facility has been constructed for a major nitric acid factory. Preparation for the transition from coal to natural-gas firing in a large power station has been completed. This measure will reduce SO_2 emissions by 30,000 tonnes per year with effect from mid-1989.

In **Canada,** Ontario Hydro has initiated a 2.5 billion dollar programme involving the retrofit of scrubbers on its largest generating stations.

In **Denmark,** the first flue-gas desulphurization (FGD) unit in a power plant will be put into operation in 1989.

The newest 250 MW_e block of **Finland's** largest coal-fired plant (1000 MW_e) has been retrofitted with a semi-dry FGD plant. A new FGD method produces elementary sulphur as a by-product with appreciable market value, and is now being developed further for simultaneous NO_x control.

In the **Federal Republic of Germany,** nearly all coal-fired power plants in operation have been retrofitted with FGD equipment (28,000 MW_e hard coal and 11,000 MW_e lignite). Most oil-fired plants were switched to low-sulphur fuels. As regards NO_x emissions, the retrofitting of existing power plants was nearly completed in 1988. The process employed for flue-gas cleaning in coal-fired power plants is selective catalytic reduction (SCR) with ammonia. At the end of 1988, plants with a total capacity of 12,000 MW_e were so equipped.

In **Norway,** all new plants have to comply with the principle of best available technology.

In **Turkey**, 40 cement-producing plants have been equipped with electrofilter systems to comply with dust emission standards.

B. Mobile sources

Within the framework of the 1958 ECE Agreement concerning the adoption of uniform conditions of approval and reciprocal recognition of approval for motor vehicles equipment and parts, the following recent modifications have been recorded:

As regards Regulation No. 49 (on emissions from diesel engines), adherence by **Finland** as of 22 May 1989;

As regards Regulation No. 15 (on engine emissions from passenger cars and light-duty vehicles equipped with a positive-ignition engine or with a compression-ignition engine), withdrawal by **Belgium, Denmark, France**, the **Federal Republic of Germany, Italy** and the **United Kingdom** as of 1 October 1989; by **Finland** as of 1 January 1990; by the **Netherlands** as of 20 June 1989; and by **Norway** as of 1 January 1989;

New Regulation No. 83 (uniform provisions concerning the approval of vehicles with regard to the emission of gaseous pollutants by the engine according to the engine fuel requirements) entered into force on 5 November 1989. As of 31 December 1989, the regulation was applicable in **France**, the **Federal Republic of Germany, Italy**, the **Netherlands**, and the **United Kingdom**.

Turkey, although not a Party to the 1958 ECE Agreement, has adopted national standards for motor vehicle emissions in accordance with the 04 amendment series of ECE Regulation No. 15.

In **Canada**, Provincial Ministers will implement by 1992 vehicle inspection and maintenance programmes in provinces where ozone problems occur. Petrol volatility will be limited to 10.5 PSI in all provinces, effective from the summer of 1990, with consideration of lower limits in provinces where ozone problems persist. At the beginning of 1990 regulations controlling petrol vapour emissions from petrol distribution and marketing activities were put in place.

In **Denmark**, emission standards corresponding to United States standards will become mandatory for all light-duty vehicles from October 1990. From October 1989 to October 1990, EEC standards for passenger cars with engines above 2 litres will be mandatory.

In **Finland**, passenger cars will have to comply with the US-83 model standards as of January 1990 for new passenger car models, and as of January 1992 for all new passenger cars. Exhaust limits for heavy-duty vehicles using diesel fuels were introduced in 1989, to be tightened further by 1995.

In **Norway**, emission standards corresponding to US-83 standards are mandatory for passenger cars from January 1989 and for diesel passenger cars from January 1990. For light-duty trucks US-90 standards will be required within 1991. For heavy duty vehicles US-91 standards will become mandatory before the end of 1993.

Sweden will introduce stringent emission control standards for heavy-duty vehicles, corresponding to 1990 United States federal standards.

The **European Economic Community** reached agreement in June 1989 on more stringent emission standards for small cars below 1.4 litres, which will become effective for new models from July 1992 onwards and for all new cars as of 31 December 1992. New test cycles for motor vehicles will be decided upon before the end of 1990.

As regards *aircraft engine emissions* of hydrocarbons, carbon monoxide and nitrogen oxides, an amendment to annex 16 (volume II: environmental protection) of the Convention on International Civil Aviation was adopted by the Council of the International Civil Aviation Organization (ICAO) in March 1988 and became applicable as of 17 November 1988. Compliance with the emission standards of annex 16/II as amended was formally confirmed to ICAO by **Austria, Denmark, Finland, Portugal, Sweden** and **Switzerland**; while **Canada**, the **Federal Republic of Germany, Italy**, the **Netherlands**, the **United Kingdom** and the **United States of America** notified ICAO of national differences with regard to these standards.

Chapter 3: ADMINISTRATIVE STRUCTURES

I. National and local authorities: responsibilities and co-ordination

In **Austria**, an Agreement on Ambient Air Quality Goals has been concluded between the federal and state governments, with a view to reducing air pollution to such a level that national air quality standards for SO_2, particulates, NO_2 and

CO are not exceeded from 31 December 1990 onwards.

In the **Byelorussian Soviet Socialist Republic**, a new State Committee for Environmental Protection was established in 1988. It is also responsible for air quality assessment and management.

In **Canada**, acid deposition as well as control programmes for NO_x and VOCs is dealt with by the Canadian Council of Resource and Environment Ministers, supported by officials on the Federal-Provincial Long-range Transport of Airborne Pollutants Steering Committee. A new Parliamentary Committee on the Environment was created in 1988 to replace the Special Parliamentary Committee on Acid Rain. The new Committee has a broad mandate to deal with acid rain and other environmental issues.

In **Portugal**, a 1988 decree established an inspection office within the General Directorate for Environmental Quality, to supervise potentially polluting activities. The inspectors have right of access to all industrial plants or other pollution sources, taking samples or supervising the calibration of equipment for pollution analysis and emissions control.

In **Turkey**, the implementation of environmental policies during the sixth Five-Year-Development Plan period (1990 to 1995) will be evaluated continuously by a new *ad hoc* expert committee whose Air Quality Subcommittee will assess air quality data, emission inventories, control strategies and technologies, and prepare amendments to the Air Pollution Control Regulations as required.

In the **Union of Soviet Socialist Republics**, draft general principles for restructuring economic and social management in the Union republics on the basis of broader sovereign rights, autonomy and self-financing were presented for public discussion in March 1989, including a section on environmental conservation and the utilization of natural resources. The Union republics will thus be entitled to make use of the common State fund for natural resources, and to adopt limits and standards with the agreement of the USSR State Committee on Environmental Protection. The costs of Union-wide environmental programmes and of participation in international programmes will be shared between the Union budget and the budgets of the republics. Revenues from the proposed system of emission charges will also be used for these purposes.

II. Monitoring systems for air quality and air pollution effects

Belgium monitors sulphur oxides and particulates at some 190 stations on a daily basis. There also exists an automatic monitoring network which measures SO_2, NO, NO_x, O_3 and CnHm at nearly 70 stations. Further local monitoring is carried out near industrial sources with high levels of atmospheric pollution.

In **Bulgaria**, monitoring of NO_x emission reductions started in 1989.

In **France**, approximately 2,000 monitoring stations are functioning at present, mainly in the vicinity of industrial plants and in cities, and gradually extending to rural areas. A 1988 ministerial circular regulates the method of automated self-monitoring for emissions from large stationary sources.

At the beginning of November 1989 the **German Democratic Republic** put a smog monitoring system into operation in its counties. In Berlin, as well as in county towns, the 24-hour sulphur dioxide average is published daily. In Berlin, these average values are taken from five automatic stations at present. In 1992 another 10 stations will start to operate. In the case of an average 24-hour level of 0.6 mg measured at two stations, the information level will be announced. In the case of 1.2 mg, level 1 will be announced and in the case of 1.8 mg at one station, level 2 will be announced. Specific recommendations and regulations have been laid down for all levels, including reductions or limitations for the production capacities of enterprises in the territory concerned, as well as traffic.

In the **Federal Republic of Germany**, a focus of monitoring efforts is on the prevention of harmful environmental impacts during weather situations with a poor exchange between atmospheric layers (smog). In this connection the Sample Smog Ordinance, drawn up by the Inter-state (*Länder*) Committee on Immission Control in 1984 and tightened in 1987, is of particular importance. The sample ordinance lays down basic principles for the smog ordinances which are to be issued by the *Länder* and adapted to the latest scientific development.

In **Luxembourg**, an automated monitoring network has been established measuring SO_2, NO, NO_2, CO, O_3, VOCs and dust.

The national routine monitoring programme in **Norway** involves measurements of SO_2, NO_x, soot, lead, sulphur particulates and fluorides.

The programme comprises 25 monitoring stations. Background concentrations of VOCs are currently measured at two stations, ozone at 14 stations, PAN at two stations, PAH at six stations, benzene at one station, and dioxins at several stations located near waste incinerators and heavy traffic areas.

In **Poland**, there is at present at least one sampling station in each provincial town and a minimum of three in cities with more than 100,000 inhabitants. All these stations are used for short-term (24 hour) measurements of SO_2 and suspended particles. Some of them also monitor levels of NO_x. For each sampling station long-term (whole year) concentrations are also calculated.

In **Portugal** there are some 80 air quality surveillance stations, most of them in the vicinity of industrial installations or in cities. There is also a national monitoring network with automatic measurement of SO_2, NO_x, CO and O_3.

The air quality monitoring network in **Spain** comprises several hundred sampling sites, 41 regional laboratories, 14 regional data centres, a national data assessment centre and a national reference laboratory. The pollutants most extensively studied are sulphur dioxide and suspended particulates. Levels of hydrocarbons, nitrogen oxides, lead, fluoride and ozone are determined additionally at some places.

In **Switzerland**, a monitoring network for photo-oxidant formation has been established in the different regions and at different altitudes. Switzerland is also considering establishing an alarm system for ozone and NO_x.

In **Turkey**, enterprises are obliged to monitor and register all emissions and wastes and to report these data to the competent authorities. Besides this monitoring obligation for individual enterprises, measurement devices for the determination of air pollution levels which were available in 28 provinces were made available in 50 provinces in 1987. At present, measurements are carried out with 67 semi-automatic pollution monitoring devices in addition to 10 fully automatic devices in Ankara.

In the **USSR** the number of cities with air quality monitoring sites is being increased to more than 540 (with air sampling at least four times a day). Monitoring is also carried out by mobile laboratories along main traffic routes. In some cities, automatic stations are being introduced to monitor atmospheric air pollution. In more than 220 cities, an alarm system has been introduced for periods of unfavourable climatic conditions contributing to the increase of pollution levels. In

such conditions, industrial enterprises shall adopt particular measures to decrease hazardous emissions into the atmosphere, and the monitoring service increases the frequency of sampling and analysis for the assessment of the effectiveness of air pollution control in enterprises.

III. Integrated assessment of costs and benefits in national decision-making

In the **Federal Republic of Germany** cost-impact and economic-impact assessments of emission reductions are carried out by the Association of the Electric Power Production Industry and by the Federal Environmental Agency. According to rough estimates, the expenditure of approximately DM 22 billion for the flue-gas cleaning programme in implementation of the Ordinance on Large Combustion Plants in the Public Power Plant sector has had a macro-economic impact on production amounting to nearly DM 60 billion, thereby safeguarding some 300,000 jobs (man years) at construction sites and suppliers. The operation of anti-pollution facilities, which is highly automated and not very labour-intensive, resulted in the creation of approximately 1,000 new jobs. The impact on electricity price levels is expected to amount to 0.013 DM/KWh on average.

In **Norway**, a model study for the assessment of policies for air quality improvements in Oslo by the year 2000 (taking into account cost-effectiveness, beneficial effects, human health and welfare, corrosion, etc.) concluded that a 90 per cent reduction of adverse effects caused by air pollution would be feasible.

In **Turkey**, a recent assessment quantified the expected expenditures for pollution control facilities to be installed in existing thermal power plants, and their impact on the unit cost of electricity.

IV. The role of research and development

Belgium reports that research projects are currently under way for coal desulphurization and for methods to reduce odours.

In **Canada**, the Federal Government has set aside $Can 25 million as its share of the costs of commercial technology demonstration projects for air pollution abatement at smelters. About $Can 3 million per year are directed towards the research and development of emission control technologies for power plants, through various federal departments. Final reports of the federal-provincial programme on the long-range transport of air pollutants will be available in April 1990.

For five years the **Finnish** National acidification project (HAPRO) studied the effects of emissions from fuel use and other sources on Finnish nature. The results of the project shall be published in 1990. Preliminary results indicate that the internationally proposed critical levels for nitrogen and sulphur deposition are being exceeded over almost the whole country and that the most sensitive bio-indicators have reacted. The Government has proposed a new study project on global air pollution (SILMU). The project will start in 1990 with a budget of 12 million Finnish marks.

In **France**, a major new research programme on atmospheric and climatic trends (ECLAT) was launched jointly by the Ministries of the Environment and Research in December 1988.

In the **Federal Republic of Germany**, research and development projects are conducted by the federal Government in conjunction with the states, with the scientific community and industry. These projects are mainly geared towards the development of environmentally "clean" technologies, the verification and updating of ambient air quality values and the improved monitoring of air quality, in particular through an "early warning system" for smog control and research on atmospheric transport processes and chemical reactions. Effect-related research (252 projects funded in 1987) includes long-term exposure in low close-range and includes additional anthropogenic and natural influencing factors.

In the **Netherlands**, the final report of the first phase of the Dutch Priority Programme on Acidification was released in November 1988. Air pollution problems are also addressed in the "National Environmental Survey 1985-2010 (Concern for Tomorrow)" published by the National Institute of Public Health and Environmental Protection in 1988, in preparation for the 1989 National Environmental Policy Plan.

In **Portugal**, research projects are funded from an annual budget for research and development on the environment.

In **Switzerland**, in September 1988, the Federal Office for Environment, Forests and Landscape Protection published supplements to its earlier reports on anthropogenic pollutant emissions from 1950 to 2010, and on pollutant emissions by private road transport from 1950 to 2000; and in February 1989, a comprehensive report on

"Ozone in Switzerland" prepared by the Federal Commission on Air Hygiene.

In the **United States of America**, an "Assessment plan update", issued in August 1989, provides information on the state of implementation of the National Acid Precipitation Assessment Program (NAPAP) to be completed in September 1990. Over 30 reports on the state of science and technology have been prepared and will be reviewed at an international meeting at Hilton Head Island, South Carolina, in February 1990.

In **Yugoslavia**, the Federal Hydrometeorological Institute has published a report on the chemical composition of precipitation and air above Yugoslavia in the period 1982 to 1987. A methodology has been developed for the assessment of annual sulphur emissions in Yugoslavia. The Federal Fund for Stimulation of Technological Development has been used for the development of flue-gas desulphurization techniques (limestone method), with the participation of a consortium of 10 scientific institutions. Other techniques studied include absorption-desorption techniques for flue-gas desulphurization of solid fuels, desulphurization of coal before combustion, development of boilers for fluidized bed combustion and two-phased burning processes for solid, liquid and gaseous fuels.

Chapter 4: INTERNATIONAL ACTIVITIES

I. Activities within the Executive Body

As of 31 December 1989, Parties to the 1979 Convention on Long-range Transboundary Air Pollution numbered 31 States and the European Economic Community (table 4). Thirty States and the European Economic Community had also become Parties to the 1984 Protocol on Long-term Financing of the Co-operative Programme for Monitoring and Evaluation of the Long-range Transmission of Air Pollutants in Europe (EMEP), in force as of 28 January 1988; and 19 States had become Parties to the 1985 Protocol on the Reduction of Sulphur Emissions or their Transboundary Fluxes by at least 30 per cent, in force as of 2 September 1987. Twenty-seven Parties had signed the 1988 Protocol concerning the Control of Nitrogen Oxide Emissions or their Transboundary Fluxes, adopted on 31 October 1988, and eight Parties had ratified the Protocol (membership of protocols is also listed in table 4).

II. Other bilateral and multilateral activities in the ECE region

A bilateral environmental agreement concluded in 1987 between **Austria** and **Czechoslovakia**, and including air-pollution control, entered into force in April 1989.

In November 1989, **Canada** and the **Union of Soviet Socialist Republics** signed an environmental agreement as well as three memoranda of understanding in the area of the environment. The Eastern Canadian Control Program has already resulted in a 33 per cent reduction of the yearly transboundary fluxes of SO_2 towards the north eastern **United States**. This export of Canadian emissions will be less than half of the 1980 level, with full implementation of the programme in 1994.

In May 1989, **Czechoslovakia** hosted a conference of members of government responsible for environmental questions, including **Austria**, **Hungary**, the **German Democratic Republic**, the **Federal Republic of Germany**, **Poland**, the **Union of Soviet Socialist Republics** and the **European Economic Community**. The conference agreed on further bilateral and multilateral co-operation, *inter alia*, to elaborate and implement technical and technological measures to reduce air pollution.

Czechoslovakia, the **German Democratic Republic** and **Poland** signed a tripartite agreement for co-operation in the field of environmental protection at Wroclaw (Poland) in July 1989. Article 9 of the agreement deals with air pollution monitoring and abatement in common border regions, with specific reference to the Convention.

A bilateral action programme on air pollution was signed between **Finland** and the **Union of Soviet Socialist Republics** in October 1989 in Helsinki. The agreement for the abatement of transboundary air pollution in border regions refers to the Convention and its protocols, and includes, *inter alia*, specific obligations for a 50 per cent reduction of sulphur emissions from the 1982 level by the end of 1995 at the latest, a stabilization of nitrogen oxide emissions at their 1987 level by 1994, and a reduction of heavy metal emissions by using best economically available technology.

The **Federal Republic of Germany** signed bilateral agreements on environmental co-operation, including provisions for air-pollution control, with the **Union of Soviet Socialist Republics** in October 1988, with **Hungary** in December 1988, and with **Bulgaria** in April 1989.

The **Netherlands** signed a bilateral agreement on environmental co-operation, including provisions for air-pollution control, with **Hungary** in December 1988.

The **European Economic Community** (EEC) participates with the International Atomic Energy Agency (IAEA) and the World Meteorological Organization (WMO) in a research programme to validate long-range transport models for atmospheric pollutants in Europe (ATMES). The Programme was initiated by the IAEA International Nuclear Safety Advisory Group, as part of the response to the Chernobyl nuclear plant accident and the 1986 Convention on Early Notification of a Nuclear Accident.

At the economic summit meeting held in Paris in July 1989, the EEC Commission was requested to co-ordinate assistance to **Hungary** and **Poland** in the economic and environmental field, including air pollution abatement technology, in the context of the PHARE programme (*Pologne-Hongrie: aide à la réforme économique*).

In November 1989, the *Nordic Council of Ministers* adopted a common Nordic action plan against air pollution. The plan contains common Nordic goals, strategies and measures for the reduction of emissions of SO_2, NO_x, photochemical oxidants, CFCs, halons, CO_2 and other gases affecting the climate. The Nordic countries will prepare national action plans for different areas such as transport and energy production and consumption in order to reach these goals.

The concluding document of the Vienna follow-up meeting to the *Conference on Security and Co-operation in Europe*, adopted on 10 January 1989, specifically addressed co-operation on long-range transboundary air pollution within the framework of the Convention. The participating States called upon Contracting Parties and Signatories to the Convention to become parties to the Protocol on the Reduction of Sulphur Emissions or their Transboundary Fluxes by at least 30 per cent, and recommended further steps to reduce sulphur emissions. They welcomed the adoption of the Protocol concerning the Control of Emissions of Nitrogen Oxides, and recognized the need to develop arrangements to reduce emissions of other relevant air pollutants such as hydrocarbons and those producing photochemical oxidants. They agreed to strengthen and develop EMEP, *inter alia* by extending and improving the system of monitoring stations, by providing EMEP with the necessary information regarding emissions of pollutants, by further developing comparable methods of measurement, and by expanding coverage to include other relevant air pollutants, in particular nitrogen oxides, hydrocarbons and photochemical oxidants.

The *Baltic Marine Environment Protection Commission* (HELCOM) signed a memorandum of understanding with the ECE secretariat in August 1989, for co-operation with regard to data on airborne pollution in the Baltic Sea area. Following a request by the *Paris Commission for the Prevention of Marine Pollution from Land-based Sources* (PARCOM), a similar agreement with ECE concerning data on airborne pollution in the North Sea area is now in preparation.

A *Consultative Meeting for the Protection of the Arctic Environment*, hosted by **Finland** at Rovaniemi in September 1989, included discussions on air pollution monitoring, effects and controls in the Arctic region.

Non-governmental initiatives relevant to the implementation of the Convention included a seminar on *integrated pollution control in Europe and North America*, organized by the Institute for European Environmental Policy in Brussels (Belgium) in November 1988; an *international conference on critical loads*, organized by the Environmental Law Institute in Washington, D.C. (USA) in April 1989; and a conference on the establishment of an European Forum for Forest Protection, organized jointly by the Inter-Action Council and the Polish Academy of Sciences in Cracow (Poland) in June 1989.

III. Global aspects and concerns

As a result of initiatives by both the *1987 International Conference on the Protection of the North Sea* and the *Baltic Marine Environment Protection Commission*, the *International Maritime Organization* (IMO) has included the question of air pollution from ships in the work programme of its Marine Environment Protection Committee, starting with the development of environmentally sound standards for marine fuels at the 27th session of the Committee in March 1989.

Growing international concern over potential climatic change as a result of fossil fuel combustion and emissions of carbon dioxide and other gases producing greenhouse effects led to the establishment of a joint WMO/UNEP *Intergovernmental Panel on Climate Change* (IPCC), which held its first session in Geneva in November 1988 and a second session in Nairobi in June 1989. By Resolution 43/53 on the protection of climate for present and future generations of mankind, the United Nations General Assembly called upon Governments and all relevant organizations and programmes of the United Nations system to support the work of the IPCC. The United Nations Economic Commission for Europe, at its forty-fourth session in April 1989, decided to undertake a review of the Commission's programmes, activities and discussions bearing on the relationship of human activities and the climate, also taking into account the work and studies of the IPCC and possible ECE contributions thereto.

TABLE 1

TOTAL SO2 EMISSIONS 1980-2005 IN THE ECE REGION
(In thousands of tonnes S per year)

	1980	1981	1982	1983	1984	1985	1986	1987	1988a/	1989a/	1990b/	1993b/	1995b/	2000b/	2005b/
Austria	185			109		89		68	57		47		40	39	
Belgium	414	356	347	280	250	226	237	207			210		215		
Bulgaria	517			570				535	515						
Byelorussian SSR c/	370	365	355	355	345	345	345	345	329	298	292	260	246	228	200
Canada	2322					1843					1881		1526	1535	1549
Czech and Slovak Federal Republic	1550					1575	1510	1480	1400						
Denmark	224	182	184	156	148	170	139	125	121		133		95	88	
Finland	292	268	244	187	184	191	166	164	151		126			133	
France	1669	1294	1245	1047	933	735	671	645	613	667					
German Democratic Republic	2132	2158	2775	2318	2519	2670	2679	2803	2629	2621					
Germany, Federal Republic of d/	1605	1515	1430	1355	1320	1225	1170	990	650	530					
Greece	200					250								430	
Hungary	771					702	685	646	609	542	582		571	547	
Iceland	3				3	3									
Ireland	110				70	69		80	74		107		126		
Italy	1900			1575	1328	1252	1185	1205							
Liechtenstein	*				*						*				
Luxembourg	12			7		8					5				
Netherlands e/	233			167		138	138	141	138	127					
Norway	71	64	56	52	48	49	45	38	33	33		35		53	
Poland f/	2050					2150	2100	2100	2090		2250			1450	
Portugal g/	133			153		99	117	109	102		106	135	139	152	
Romania	900									900					
Spain	1625					1095									
Sweden h/	257								107		102	95	90	91	96
Switzerland	63				48						31		29	30	32
Turkey	1925				138	161	177								
Ukrainian SSR c/	1925					1732	1696	1632	1606	1536	1495	1350	1170	1105	870
USSR i/	6400	6309	6237	5700	5926	5555	5925	5452	5062	4659	4790	4550	4410	4110	3700
United Kingdom	2424	2194	2082	1909	1837	1838	1929	1932	1832		1916	1763	1621	1223	1009
USA	11950	11750	11000	10750	11050	10800	10600	10200							
Yugoslavia	650	650	650	700	725	750	750	775	800	825					
EEC k/						6813									

Notes: * <0.5

a/ Preliminary data
b/ Projected estimates
c/ Also included under USSR
d/ 2000 = 1998 estimates
e/ 1985 = 1994 estimates; 2000 estimates: According to national environmental policy plan
f/ 1990 estimates: Not taking into account planned abatement measures
g/ For the years 1990, 1993, 1995 and 2000 emissions of small combustion plants were not calculated
h/ Projections based on current administrative regulations
i/ European part of USSR within EMEP
k/ CORINAIR total, based on separate inventory of 12 EEC member states

TABLE 2

TOTAL NOx EMISSIONS 1980-2005 IN THE ECE REGION
(In thousands of tonnes NO2 per year)

	1980	1981	1982	1983	1984	1985	1986	1987	1988a/	1989a/	1990b/	1993b/	1995b/	2000b/	2005b/
Austria	233			228		230		218	212		201		171	155	
Belgium	442				295	281	292	297			300		250		
Bulgaria					150		150	150	150						
Byelorussian SSR c/	244	235	235	231	226	220	258	287	310	263	271	269	251	187	159
Canada	1959					1887					1923		1864	1929	1995
Czech and Slovak Federal Republic	1204					1127	1060	965	950	950					
Denmark	241	208	224	218	225	258	266	262	249		254		224	177	
Finland d/	264	248	245	236	233	251	256	270	276				321	226	193
France	1823	1701	1688	1645	1632	1615	1618	1630	1615	1772					
German Democratic Republic						746		701	708	705					
Germany, Federal Republic of e/	2970	2880	2870	2880	2980	2930	2990	2940	2860					1980	
Greece															
Hungary	273					262	268	276	259	249	264		280	279	
Iceland	13				12	12									
Ireland	67				66	68	77	77	77		109		123		
Italy	1480				1568	1595	1607	1700							
Liechtenstein	*				*										
Luxembourg	23			21		19					15				
Netherlands	548					544			552	552				268	
Norway	184	178	180	190	206	203	222	232	227	226				155	
Poland						1500	1530	1520	1550						
Portugal f/	166			192		96	110	116	122		142	173	187	193	
Romania															
Spain	950					950									
Sweden g/	398					394			390		373		343	341	347
Switzerland	196				214						184		138	127	123
Turkey															
Ukrainian SSR c/						1059	1112	1095	1090	1065	1099	1096	1056	930	885
USSR h/	3167	3515	3560	3510	3396	3369	3330	4214	4190						
United Kingdom	2418	2328	2321	2230	2162	2278	2350	2429	2480		2573	2471	2300	1822	1718
USA	20300	20300	19500	19100	19700	19700	19300	19500					19100		
Yugoslavia	350	360	370	370	380	400	420	440	480						
EEC i/						10428									

Notes: * <0.5

a/ Preliminary data

b/ Projected estimates

c/ Also included under USSR

d/ 2005 = 2010 estimates; 2000 and 2010 projections by Nitrogen Oxide Commission

e/ 2000 = 1998 estimates

f/ For the years 1990, 1993, 1995 and 2000 emissions of small combustion plants were not calculated

g/ Projections based on current environmental regulations

h/ European part of USSR within EMEP

i/ CORINAIR total, based on separate inventory of 12 EEC member states

TABLE 3

TOTAL VOC EMISSIONS 1980-2005 IN THE ECE REGION
(In thousands of tonnes HC per year)

	1980	1981	1982	1983	1984	1985	1986	1987	1988a/	1989a/	1990b/	1993b/	1995b/	2000b/	2005b/
Austria	382					441		474	466		449		366	305	
Belgium	374														
Bulgaria c/		2594						2594							
Byelorussian SSR d/	549	546	543	543	540	516	506	509	535	511	508	496	442	330	273
Canada e/	1871					1783					1734		1723	1785	1892
Czech and Slovak Federal Republic															
Denmark	197					184									
Finland f/	130					181									
France f/				2150		2874								1314	
German Democratic Republic	84	98	103	107	114	127	134	140	157	138					
Germany, Federal Republic of g/	2530	2450	2430	2420	2430	2430	2470	2460	2450						
Greece						657									
Hungary															
Iceland															
Ireland						110									
Italy															
Liechtenstein	*														
Luxembourg															
Netherlands h/		488				450		480	476	473				198	
Norway i/	157	161	163	166	171	174	182	188	188	193					
Poland f/									700						
Portugal f/ k/	92			99		134	145	149	156		168	187	198	218	
Romania															
Spain															
Sweden l/									460				291	225	195
Switzerland	311				339						297		253	262	294
Turkey															
Ukrainian SSR d/						1626		1687	1604	1513	1500	1490	1480	1460	1440
USSR m/	7000	7372	6967	6443	6506	6639	7434	8056	7824						
United Kingdom	1781	1756	1789	1740	1729	1763	1795	1816	1846		1868	1694	1535	1222	1051
USA	23000	21600	20100	20900	21900	20300	19500	19600							
Yugoslavia															
EEC n/						19646									

Notes: * <0.5

a/ Preliminary data

b/ Projected estimates

c/ Emissions from chemical, petrochemical and other sectors of industry

d/ Also included under USSR

e/ 1980 data: Emissions of total gaseous hydrocarbons, including methane; 1985-2000 estimates: any organic compound which participates in atmospheric photochemical reactions
with the exception of methane, ethane, methylchloroform, CH_3CO_3, CFC11, CFC12, CFC22, FC23, CFC114, CFC115, HCFC123, HCFC134A, HCFC134B, HCFC141B, HCFC142B

f/ Not including natural sources

g/ 1986 data excluding methane, e.g. from mining, agriculture and landfills

h/ Including methane and agricultural non-combustion; 2000 estimates: According to national environmental policy plan

i/ Including evaporative emissions from oil/gas drilling/exploitation

k/ For the years 1990, 1993, 1995 and 2000 emissions of small combustion plants were not calculated

l/ Methane only included for mobile sources/road traffic

m/ European part of USSR within EMEP

n/ CORINAIR total, based on separate inventory of 12 EEC member states

TABLE 4

Status of the Convention on Long-range Transboundary Air Pollution and its Related Protocols (as of 31 December 1989)

	Convention (a)		EMEP Protocol (b)		SO2 Protocol (c)		NOx Protocol (d)	
	Signature	Ratification*	Signature	Ratification	Signature	Ratification	Signature	Ratification
Austria	13.11.1979	16.12.1982 (R)		4. 6.1987 (Ac)	9. 7.1985	4. 6.1987 (R)	1.11.1988	
Belgium	13.11.1979	15. 7.1982 (R)	25. 2.1985	5. 8.1987 (R)	9. 7.1985	9. 6.1989 (R)	1.11.1988	30. 3.1989 (R)
Bulgaria	14.11.1979	9. 6.1981 (R)	4. 4.1985	26. 9.1986 (Ap)	9. 7.1985	26. 9.1986 (Ap)	1.11.1988	8. 6.1989 (At)
Byelorussian SSR	14.11.1979	13. 6.1980 (R)	28. 9.1984	4.10.1985 (At)	9. 7.1985	10. 9.1986 (At)	1.11.1988	
Canada	13.11.1979	15.12.1981 (R)	3.10.1984	4.12.1985 (R)	9. 7.1985	4.12.1985 (R)	1.11.1988	
Czechoslovakia	13.11.1979	23.12.1983 (R)		26.11.1986 (Ac)	9. 7.1985	26.11.1986 (Ap)	1.11.1988	
Denmark	14.11.1979	18. 6.1982 (R)	28. 9.1984	29. 4.1986 (R)	9. 7.1985	29. 4.1986 (R)	1.11.1988	
Finland	13.11.1979	15. 4.1981 (R)	7.12.1984	24. 6.1986 (R)	9. 7.1985	24. 6.1986 (R)	1.11.1988	20. 7.1989 (Ap)
France	13.11.1979	3.11.1981 (Ap)	22. 2.1985	30.10.1987 (R)	9. 7.1985	13. 3.1986 (Ap)	1.11.1988	
German Democratic Republic	13.11.1979	7. 6.1982 (R)		17.12.1986 (Ac) (2)	9. 7.1985		1.11.1988	
Germany, Federal Republic of	13.11.1979	15. 7.1982 (R) (2)	26. 2.1985	7.10.1986 (R) (2)	9. 7.1985	3. 3.1987 (R) (2)	1.11.1988	
Greece	14.11.1979	30. 8.1983 (R)		24. 6.1988 (Ac)				
Holy See	14.11.1979			8. 5.1985 (Ap)			3. 5.1989	
Hungary	13.11.1979	22. 9.1980 (R)	27. 3.1985		9. 7.1985	11. 9.1986 (R)	1. 5.1989	
Iceland	13.11.1979	5. 5.1983 (R)		26. 6.1987 (R)			1.11.1988	
Ireland	13.11.1979	15. 7.1982 (R)	4. 4.1985	12. 1.1989 (R)			1.11.1988	
Italy	14.11.1979	15. 7.1982 (R)	28. 9.1984	1. 5.1985 (Ac)	9. 7.1985	13. 2.1986 (R)	1.11.1988	
Liechtenstein	14.11.1979	22.11.1983 (R)		24. 8.1987 (R)	9. 7.1985	24. 8.1987 (R)	1.11.1988	11.10.1989 (At) (3)
Luxembourg	13.11.1979	15. 7.1982 (R)	21.11.1984	22.10.1985 (At) (3)	9. 7.1985	30. 4.1986 (At) (3)	1.11.1988	11.10.1989 (R)
Netherlands	13.11.1979	15. 7.1982 (At) (3)	28. 9.1984	12. 3.1985 (At)	9. 7.1985	4.11.1986 (R)	1.11.1988	
Norway	13.11.1979	13. 2.1981 (R)	28. 9.1984	14. 9.1988 (Ac)	9. 7.1985		1.11.1988	
Poland	13.11.1979	19. 7.1985 (R) (2)		10. 1.1989 (Ac)			1.11.1988	
Portugal	14.11.1979	29. 9.1980 (R)						
Romania	14.11.1979 (1)							
San Marino	14.11.1979							
Spain	14.11.1979	15. 6.1982 (R)	28. 9.1984	11. 8.1987 (Ac)			1.11.1988	
Sweden	13.11.1979	12. 2.1981 (R)	3.10.1984	12. 8.1985 (R)	9. 7.1985	31. 3.1986 (R)	1.11.1988	24. 7.1989 (At)
Switzerland	13.11.1979	6. 5.1983 (R)	3.10.1984	26. 7.1985 (R)	9. 7.1985	21. 9.1987 (R)	1.11.1988	21. 6.1989 (At)
Turkey	13.11.1979	18. 4.1983 (R)	28. 9.1984	20.12.1985 (R)		2.10.1986 (At)	1.11.1988	
Ukrainian SSR	14.11.1979	5. 6.1980 (R)	28. 9.1984	30. 8.1985 (At)	9. 7.1985	10. 9.1986 (At)	1.11.1988	
USSR	13.11.1979	22. 5.1980 (R)	20.11.1984	21. 8.1985 (At)	9. 7.1985		1.11.1988	
United Kingdom	13.11.1979	15. 7.1982 (R) (4)	28. 9.1984	12. 8.1985 (R)				
USA	13.11.1979	30.11.1981 (At)		29.10.1984 (At)			1.11.1988	13. 7.1989 (At)
Yugoslavia	13.11.1979	18. 3.1987 (R)	28. 9.1984	28.10.1987 (Ac)				
European Community	14.11.1979	15. 7.1982 (Ap)		17. 7.1986 (Ap)			1.11.1988 (1)	
Total:	35	32	22	31	21	19	27	8

*R = Ratification
Ac = Accession
Ap = Approval
At = Acceptance

(1) With a declaration upon signature
(2) With a declaration upon ratification
(3) For the Kingdom in Europe
(4) Including the Bailiwick of Jersey, the Bailiwick of Guernsey, the Isle of Man, Gibraltar, the United Kingdom Sovereign Base Areas of Akrotiri and Dhekhelia in the Island of Cyprus

(a) = Convention of Long-range Transboundary Air Pollution, adopted 13.11.1979, entry into force 16.3.1983
(b) = Protocol to the 1979 Convention on Long-range Transboundary Air Pollution on Long-term Financing of the Co-operative Programme for Monitoring and Evaluation of the Long-range Transmission of Air Pollutants in Europe (EMEP), adopted 28.9.1984, entry into force 28.1.1988
(c) = Protocol to the 1979 Convention on Long-range Transboundary Air Pollution on the Reduction of Sulphur Emissions or their Transboundary Fluxes by at least 30 percent, adopted 8.7.1985, entry into force 2.9.1987
(d) = Protocol to the 1979 Convention on Long-range Transboundary Air Pollution concerning the Control of Emissions of Nitrogen Oxides or their Transboundary Fluxes, adopted 31.10.1988

Part TWO

THE 1988 FOREST DAMAGE SURVEY IN EUROPE

Executive Summary

The report on the 1988 Forest Damage Survey in Europe is the third to be issued by the Programme Task Force of the *International Co-operative Programme on Assessment and Monitoring of Air Pollution Effects on Forests*. It summarizes the results of forest health surveys conducted in 1988 in 25 European countries. The report also reflects progress made within the Programme Task Force in harmonizing the methods of forest damage assessment among the participating countries who based their assessment procedures on the ECE Manual, adopted by the Programme Task Force in 1986 as a common standard for conducting forest damage surveys. The manual specifies that defoliation of sample trees (loss of needles or leaves) due to biotic or abiotic causes shall be classified as follows:

class 0:	needle/leaf loss < 10%	- no defoliation
class 1:	needle/leaf loss 11-25%	- slight defoliation
class 2:	needle/leaf loss 26-60%	- moderate defoliation
class 3:	needle/leaf loss > 60%	- severe defoliation
class 4:		- dead tree

Of the 32 Parties to the Convention, 30 countries and the European Community participate in the International Co-operative Programme for the Assessment and Monitoring of Air Pollution Effects on Forests. From 1987 to 1988, the number of countries conducting forest damage surveys in conformity with the ECE Manual increased from 22 to 25 (see table 1); also, more countries are now conducting full-scale national surveys. In the USSR a new national focal centre was established in the Lithuanian SSR which will assist in starting forest damage surveys in the neighbouring Soviet Republics. Thus, results were received for the first time for coniferous forests in Estonia. In 1988, surveys at the national level were conducted for the first time by Greece, Norway, Poland and Portugal. On the other hand it must not be overlooked that for some countries which have replaced earlier denser networks, used in the

regional surveys, by the 16 x 16 km network as prescribed by the European Community or as used in eastern Europe, the results reported may be insufficient for an adequate interpretation at the national level. This applies particularly to less forested countries.

Canada and the United States co-operate with the ICP, and are conducting major research programmes in North America.

Of 161 million hectares (ha) of forests in Europe (excluding most of the forests in the USSR), around 108 million ha or roughly 65 per cent were covered in the 1988 survey. Over 990,000 trees were assessed on 53,000 sample plots. Areas not yet entirely covered by the survey include parts of some broadleaved forests, mostly in Scandinavia, and the low broadleaved evergreens (*maquis*) in Mediterranean countries where they contribute to the total forest area.

Important figures and numerical results are listed in tables 2 to 14. Table 2 gives an overview of participating countries, forest areas, density of grids and extent of survey activities. Tables 3 to 5 contain results for all species and species groups (conifers and broadleaves). Data for individual species, i.e., for spruce, pine, fir, beech and oak, are listed in tables 6 to 10. They reflect the health of forests at the species level and also indicate which countries and age groups are most affected.

Tables 11, 12 and 13 show ratings for all species (table 11), conifers (table 12) and broadleaves (table 13) of each country. These ratings are based on the proportion of sample trees in defoliation classes 2-4 (i.e. showing more than 25 per cent needle/leaf loss). It must be emphasized that it is extremely difficult to draw comparisons between the data collected by different countries. Despite the high level of harmonization that has now been achieved between the different countries, important differences remain. In addition, it is clear that the condition of European forests is determined by a variety of abiotic and biotic factors. The relative importance of these varies between regions, and similar ratings in tables 11 to 13 can result from very different causes.

Species groups

Results for **all species** are available for 25 countries/regions. Defoliation is lowest in Portugal, USSR-Lithuania, Austria, Italy-Bolzano, France, Spain, Hungary, and Bulgaria. Defoliation is intermediate in Yugoslavia, Luxembourg, Belgium-Flanders, Sweden, Switzerland, the German Democratic Republic, the Federal Republic of Germany, Finland, Greece, Liechtenstein, Denmark, the Netherlands, and Italy-Tuscany. It is highest in Poland, the United Kingdom, and Czechoslovakia (table 11).

Results for **conifers** show that defoliation is lowest in Portugal, USSR-Lithuania, Austria, Ireland, Italy-Bolzano, Bulgaria, Spain, Greece, USSR-Estonia, France, and Hungary. It is intermediate in Belgium-Flanders, Belgium-Wallonia, Luxembourg, Sweden, the Federal Republic of Germany, the Netherlands, Switzerland, Italy-Tuscany, the German Democratic Republic, Finland and Yugoslavia. Defoliation is highest in Norway, Denmark, Liechtenstein, Poland, the United Kingdom and Czechoslovakia (table 12).

Results for **broadleaves** show that defoliation is lowest in Portugal, USSR-Lithuania, Italy-Bolzano, Liechtenstein, Sweden, France, Spain, Hungary, Switzerland, Poland, Finland, Austria, Bulgaria, the German Democratic Republic, Yugoslavia, and Belgium-Flanders. It is intermediate in Belgium-Flanders, Luxembourg, Denmark, and the Federal Republic of Germany. It is highest in the United Kingdom, Italy-Tuscany, the Netherlands, Greece and Czechoslovakia (table 13).

Species and age groups

As a result of extended survey activities, particularly in Mediterranean countries, national reports present results not only for the three main conifers (spruce, pine, fir) and the two main broadleaves (beech and oak) but also for a variety of other conifers and broadleaves. The species list in the report now comprises 25 coniferous and 34 broadleaved species.

There have been few dramatic changes in the intensity of defoliation at the species level except for oak.

In general, the health of **Norway spruce** recovered slightly in most countries. However, in the age group of trees over 60 years old, which in all countries is considerably more defoliated than the group of trees under 60 years, defoliation (classes 2 to 4) ranges from 12 to 44 per cent in 11 out of 19 reporting countries. The health of **Scots pine** recovered in some countries but deteriorated in others. In the age group over 60 years, defoliation exceeds 10 per cent in 11 out of 21 reporting countries. **Fir** recovered in most of the 10 reporting countries but remains the most affected species, with the percentage of defoliated trees in the age group over 60 years exceeding 10 per cent in seven countries and reaching as high as 38 per cent in Tuscany and 64 per cent in the Federal Republic of Germany (tables 6 to 8).

In the broadleaves, **common beech** recovered in several countries, probably due to the decline in *Rhynchaenus fagi* attack. However, defoliation still exceeded 10 per cent in 7 out of 18 reporting countries. Defoliation of **oak** increased further in many countries and has reached critical levels for moderately to severely defoliated trees in Austria (18 per cent), Belgium (23 per cent), Czechoslovakia (40 per cent), the Federal Republic of Germany (30 per cent), Luxembourg (14 per cent), the Netherlands (49 per cent) and the United Kingdom (63 per cent) in the age group older than 60 years. But Mediterranean oaks (*Quercus ilex* and *Quercus frainetto*) also show a considerable level of defoliation in Tuscany, Greece and Spain (see tables 9 and 10).

Changes in **conifer** defoliation of 5 percentage points or more between 1987 and 1988 occurred in Belgium-Flanders (+ 6.1 percentage points), Sweden (+ 6.7 percentage points), Luxembourg (+ 7.3 percentage points) and Czechoslovakia (+ 11.4 percentage points), while defoliation decreased in USSR-Lithuania (- 11.8 percentage points).

In the **broadleaves**, health deteriorated by 5.7 percentage points in Bulgaria mainly on account of insect attack. The Bulgarian experts point out that these insects had previously been considered of secondary importance; however they are developing virulent populations with highly damaging effects. Improvements of 6.0 percentage points are reported by Belgium-Flanders and Denmark, of 6.9 percentage points by Spain. The decrease of 8.0 percentage points in defoliated trees in Switzerland is attributed to the recovery of **beech** due to a marked decline of *Rhynchaenus fagi* attack and "healing" after severe late frosts in the spring of 1987 (see table 14).

The statements made in the 1987 forest damage report on the higher risk in old stands and in high elevation forests are still valid. In the Federal Republic of Germany, several thousand hectares of forests on mountain tops are expected to die in the next 5 to 10 years. The situation will probably be even more serious in the mountain regions of Czechoslovakia, and Poland.

Regional patterns

The figures in tables 11 to 13 clearly indicate that the percentage of defoliation is high in central and eastern Europe and also in some countries in north-western and south-eastern Europe. More than 10 per cent of trees (all species) are moderately to severely defoliated (classes 2-4) in 15 countries/regions: Luxembourg, Belgium-Flanders, Sweden, Switzerland, the German Democratic Republic, the Federal Republic of Germany, Finland, Greece, Liechtenstein, Denmark, the Netherlands, Italy-Tuscany, Poland, the United Kingdom, and Czechoslovakia.

The role of air pollution

In Austria, Belgium-Wallonia, Czechoslovakia, the German Democratic Republic, the Federal Republic of Germany, Italy-Tuscany, Liechtenstein, Poland, Switzerland and Yugoslavia, air pollution is considered an **essential** factor in the determination of the quality of forest stands. Forest ecosystems are negatively affected by depositions of sulphur dioxide, nitrogen compounds and their atmospheric transformation products, acids and ozone. Forest management decisions are strongly influenced by air pollution risks.

Air pollution is regarded as one of the factors **contributing** to the weakening of forest health in Belgium-Flanders, Bulgaria, the Netherlands, Denmark, Finland, France, Hungary, Italy-Bolzano, Sweden and the United Kingdom. In Hungary, biotic and abiotic causes are considered as the main damaging factors, but the effects of air pollution cannot be ignored. In Greece, biotic and abiotic factors and inadequate management practices are considered as the main parameters determining forest health.

Differences in the spatial and temporal development of forest damage became particularly evident in 1988. They support the opinion of many scientists that forest decline can best be described as a process of high causal complexity, involving both abiotic and biotic factors. In many cases air pollution is considered to play an essential role. However, it is evident that the influence and effects of the factors affecting forest condition are subject to wide variations in time and space.

The results of the 1988 forest damage survey show that:

Despite considerable differences in forest structure, species composition, levels and types of air pollution, surveys of forest health according to a commonly agreed method are now being conducted annually in 25 countries across Europe.

Forest damage, expressed as loss of needles or leaves, has been observed in all of the 25 countries. Ten countries consider air pollution the major destabilizing factor of forest health. The majority of the remaining 15 countries considers air pollution as a factor contributing to the weakening of forest health.

In many regions forests at higher elevations and forests older than 60 years continue to be considerably more defoliated than younger stands and forests at lower elevations. Several thousand hectares of forests are expected to die in the next five to ten years on hilltops in the Federal Republic of Germany. Similar conditions prevail in Czechoslovakia and Poland.

Old spruce, fir and oak are presently the most affected species with the percentage of moderately to severely defoliated trees exceeding 10 per cent in eight of the reporting countries.

The overall situation of forests in Europe indicates a clear need for continued monitoring. A continuation of the present pollution load for extended periods of time or an increase in pollution levels will threaten the vitality of forests over large areas of Europe. A reduction of the air pollution load would improve the condition of forests and postpone a possible expansion of forest decline. The important role of forests in soil and water management and the threat of global warming due to the possible greenhouse effect support the need for further action. It therefore is the opinion of the Programme Task Force that further measures to reduce air pollution are necessary.

Tables

Table 1. Parties to the Convention on Long-Range Transboundary Air Pollution, and their forest damage survey activities in 1988 (at the national level [N], regionally in selected areas [R], transnational survey [T]).

Parties to the Convention	Forest damage survey activities			
	none	national level	regional selected areas	trans-national survey
Austria		N		
Belgium (Flanders + Wallonia)			R(2)	
Bulgaria		N		
Byelorussian SSR	—			
Canada**	—			
Czechoslovakia		N		
Denmark		N		
Finland		N		
France** (national and regional)		N	(R)	
German Democratic Republic		N		
Germany, Federal Republic of		N		
Greece		N		
Hungary		N		
Iceland	—			
Ireland		N		
Italy (Bolzano + Tuscany)			R(2)	
Liechtenstein		N		
Luxembourg		N		
Netherlands		N		
Norway		N		
Poland		N		
Portugal		N		
Spain		N		
Sweden		N		
Switzerland		N		
Turkey	—			
Ukrainian SSR	—			
United Kingdom		N		
USA**	—			
USSR (Estonia + Lithuania)			R(2)	
Yugoslavia			R	
European Community*				T
32	6	21	4	1

* 12 members of the European Community submitted their results to the Commission of the EC for a transnational study.
** see national reports

Table 2. Forests and surveys in European countries.

Participating countries	Total area (1000 ha)	Forest area (1000 ha)	Coniferous forest (1000 ha)	Broadleaved forest (1000 ha)	Area surveyed (1000 ha)	Grid size (km x km)	No. of sample plots	No. of sample trees
Austria	8385	3754	3040	714	2968	$4^2/2^2$	2262	71408
Belgium–Flanders**	1373	115	54	61	115	8x8	46	1104
Belgium–Wallonia**	1684	487	248	239	487	16x16	21	1259
Bulgaria	11100	3627	1060	2567	3627	16x16	198	4600
Czechoslovakia	12789	4578	2942	1636	4578	16x16	210	12224
Denmark	4300	466	308	158	466	16x16	21	456
Finland	30464	20059	18484	1575	18484		450	3977
France	54919	14440	4840	9600	14440	$16\times1/16^2$	187	4468
German Democratic Republic*	10833	2955	2275	680	2653	varying	2604	78120
Germany, Federal Republic of	24729	7360	5078	2282	7360	$8\times12/4^2$	4117	132492
Greece	13204	2034	955	1080	2034	16x16	84	1980
Hungary	9304	1637	227	1410	1637	4x4	1027	17051
Ireland	6889	380	334	46	270	16x16	22	462
Italy	30126	8675	1735	6940	4735	16x16		
Italy–Bolzano**	704	307	292	15	307	4x4	239	7155
Italy–Tuscany**	2300	150	16	134	150	2x2	375	10766
Liechtenstein	16	8	6	2	8	0.5x0.5	361	4976
Luxembourg*	259	88	31	57	88	2x2	210	69550
Netherlands*	4147	311	208	103	281	1x1	2800	3482
Norway	30686	6660	5925	735	961	9x18	290	368000
Poland	31268	8654	6895	1759	8654	1x1	23500	4650
Portugal	8800	3060	1315	1745	3060	16x16	155	9218
Spain	50471	11792	5637	6155	8501	16x16	387	13993
Sweden	40800	23700	19400	4300	11000	varying	10300	8175
Switzerland	4129	1186	777	409	1186	4x4	703	
Turkey	77945	20199	9426	10773		1x1		
United Kingdom	24100	2200	1550	650	2200	16x16	75	1800
USSR–Estonia**	4510	1795	1149	646	1149	16x16	83	1988
USSR–Lithuania**	6487	1810	1064	764	1810	4x4	964	23130
Yugoslavia**	25600	9125	1210	7915	4889	$4^2/16^2$	2106	50400
TOTAL	529317	161155	96173	65001	108098	varying	53797	906884

sources: ECE/FAO (Rome 1985) and country reports 1988
* defoliation and discolouration combined
** regional survey

Table 3. Defoliation in **all species** (all ages; by classes and aggregates).

Participating countries	Forest area (1000 ha)	No. of sample trees	0 none	1 slight	2 moderate	3+4 severe and dead	2+3+4	1+2+3+4
Austria	3754	71408	71.2	25.2	3.0	0.6	3.6	28.8
Belgium–Fland. **	115	1104	53.8	35.8	8.7	1.7	10.4	46.2
Belgium–Wall. **	487	1259	only conifers assessed					
Bulgaria	3627	4600	59.0	33.6	6.6	0.8	7.4	43.0
Czechoslovakia	4578	12224	29.5	43.1	22.0	5.4	27.4	70.5
Denmark	466	456	51.0	31.0	13.0	5.0	18.0	49.0
Finland	20059	3977	61.2	22.7	14.2	1.9	16.1	38.8
France	14440	4468	77.3	15.8	6.0	0.9	6.9	22.7
German Democratic Republic*	2955	78120	55.6	30.6	11.1	2.7	13.8	44.4
Germany, Federal Republic of	7360	132492	47.6	37.5	14.0	0.9	14.9	52.4
Greece	2034	1980	36.0	47.0	15.9	1.1	17.0	64.0
Hungary	1637	17051	78.5	14.0	4.1	3.4	7.5	21.5
Ireland	380	462	only conifers assessed					
Italy–Bolzano **	307	7155	79.8	15.0	4.6	0.6	5.2	20.2
Italy–Tuscany **	150	10766	48.9	32.4	17.0	1.7	18.7	51.1
Liechtenstein	8		50.0	33.0			17.0	50.0
Luxembourg *	88	4976	57.6	32.1	9.3	1.0	10.3	42.4
Netherlands	311	69550	52.4	29.3	15.0	3.3	18.3	47.6
Norway	6660	3482	only conifers assessed					
Poland	8654	368000	50.6	29.0	17.0	3.4	20.4	49.4
Portugal	3060	4650	96.5	2.2	0.7	0.6	1.3	3.5
Spain	11792	9218	68.6	24.4	6.0	1.0	7.0	31.4
Sweden	23700	13993	61.3	28.1	9.4	1.2	10.6	38.7
Switzerland	1186	8175	57.0	31.0	10.0	2.0	12.0	43.0
Turkey	20199							
United Kingdom	2200	1800	36.0	39.0	21.0	4.0	25.0	64.0
USSR–Estonia **	1795	1988	48.0	43.0	8.0	1.0	9.0	52.0
USSR–Lithuania**	1810	23130	79.0	18.0	3.0	0.0	3.0	21.0
Yugoslavia **	9125	50400	67.6	22.4	7.7	2.3	10.0	32.4

sources: ECE/FAO (Rome 1985) and country reports 1988

* defoliation and discolouration combined

** regional survey

Table 4. Defoliation in **coniferous** forests (all ages; by classes and aggregates).

Participating countries	Coniferous forest (1000 ha)	No. of sample trees	0 none	1 slight	2 moderate	3+4 severe and dead	2+3+4	1+2+3+4
Austria****	3040	67974	72.4	24.3	2.7	0.6	3.3	27.6
Belgium–Flanders**	54	557	53.3	35.9	9.0	1.8	10.8	46.7
Belgium–Wallonia**	248	1374	65.0	24.0	7.0	4.0	11.0	35.0
Bulgaria	1060	2600	53.8	38.5	7.3	0.4	7.7	46.2
Czechoslovakia	2942	9687	29.0	44.0	21.6	5.4	27.0	71.0
Denmark	308	271	65.0	14.0	14.0	7.0	21.0	35.0
Finland	18484	3604	60.5	22.5	14.9	2.1	17.0	39.5
France	4840	1797	72.7	18.2	8.0	1.1	9.1	27.3
German Democratic Republic*	2003	67410	51.4	33.1	12.6	2.9	15.5	48.6
Germany, Federal Republic of	5078	88240	50.6	35.4	13.2	0.8	14.0	49.4
Greece	955	1096	49.0	43.3	6.8	0.9	7.7	51.0
Hungary	227	2293	74.0	16.6	7.3	2.1	9.4	26.0
Ireland***	334	462	69.9	25.3	4.5	0.3	4.8	30.1
Italy–Bolzano**/****	292	6911	79.6	15.2	4.6	0.6	5.2	20.4
Italy–Tuscany**	16	2800	63.6	21.0	13.5	1.9	15.4	36.4
Liechtenstein	6	2560	42.0	35.0			23.0	58.0
Luxembourg*	31	1803	68.1	20.8	9.3	1.8	11.1	31.9
Netherlands	208	44975	60.9	24.6	12.1	2.4	14.5	39.1
Norway	5925	3482	49.7	29.5	16.8	4.0	20.8	50.3
Poland	6895	294151	42.4	33.4	20.3	3.9	24.2	57.6
Portugal	1315	1976	94.0	4.3	1.5	0.2	1.7	6.0
Spain	5637	4784	70.8	21.9	6.2	1.1	7.3	29.2
Sweden	19400	10393	55.8	31.9	10.9	1.4	12.3	44.2
Switzerland	777	5258	52.0	33.0	12.0	3.0	15.0	48.0
Turkey	9426	410						
United Kingdom	1550	1146	33.0	40.0	22.0	5.0	27.0	67.0
USSR–Estonia**	1149	1988	48.0	43.0	8.0	1.0	9.0	52.0
USSR–Lithuania**	1064	16049	75.0	22.0	3.0	0.0	3.0	25.0
Yugoslavia**	1210	7238	54.5	28.0	14.0	3.5	17.5	45.5

sources: ECE/FAO (Rome 1985) and country reports 1988

* defoliation and discoloration combined

** regional survey

*** only trees <60 years assessed

**** only trees >60 years assessed

Table 5. Defoliation in **broadleaved** forests (all ages; by classes and aggregates).

Participating countries	Broadleaved forest (1000 ha)	No. of sample trees	0 none	1 slight	2 moderate	3+4 severe and dead	2+3+4	1+2+3+4
Austria ***	714	3224	51.7	40.3	6.7	1.3	8.0	48.3
Belgium–Flanders **	61	547	54.3	35.7	8.4	1.6	10.0	45.7
Belgium–Wallonia **	239		only conifers assessed					
Bulgaria	2567	2000	66.9	27.3	5.8	1.0	6.8	34.1
Czechoslovakia	1636	2555	31.5	39.4	23.5	5.6	29.1	68.5
Denmark	158	185	30.0	56.0	13.0	1.0	14.0	70.0
Finland	1575	373	67.6	24.5	7.4	0.5	7.9	32.4
France	9600	2671	80.2	14.5	4.3	1.0	5.3	19.8
German Democratic Republic*	650	10710	66.9	24.1	6.8	2.2	9.0	33.1
Germany, Federal Republic of	2282	44252	41.5	42.0	15.7	0.8	16.5	58.5
Greece	1080	884	19.8	51.7	27.1	1.4	28.5	80.2
Hungary	1410	14758	79.4	13.6	3.7	3.3	7.0	20.6
Ireland	46		only conifers assessed					
Italy–Bolzano ***	15	244	88.5	8.6	2.5	0.4	2.9	11.5
Italy–Tuscany **	-134	7966	43.9	36.0	18.2	1.9	20.1	56.1
Liechtenstein	2	2500	68.0	27.0			5.0	32.0
Luxembourg *	57	3173	51.2	36.5	10.2	2.1	12.3	48.8
Netherlands	103	24575	36.9	37.7	20.3	5.1	25.4	63.1
Norway	735		only conifers assessed					
Poland	1759	73606	79.5	13.4	5.2	1.9	7.1	20.5
Portugal	1745	2674	93.9	5.3	0.0	0.8	0.8	6.1
Spain	6155	4434	66.2	27.0	5.8	1.0	6.8	33.8
Sweden ***	4300	3600	77.3	17.5	5.0	0.2	5.2	22.7
Switzerland	409	2917	67.0	26.0	5.0	2.0	7.0	33.0
Turkey	10773		only conifers assessed					
United Kingdom	650	654	41.0	39.0	18.0	2.0	20.0	59.0
USSR–Estonia **	646		only conifers assessed					
USSR–Lithuania **	764	7081	90.0	9.0	1.0	0.0	1.0	10.0
Yugoslavia **	7915	43162	69.7	21.3	6.7	2.3	9.0	30.3

sources: ECE/FAO (Rome 1985) and country reports 1988
* defoliation and discoloration combined
** regional survey
*** only trees >60 years assessed

Table 6. Defoliation in **spruce** (by age groups; by classes and aggregates).

Countries	Percent trees defoliated, up to 60 years old							Percent trees defoliated, >60 years old						
	No. of sample trees	0	1	2	3+4	2–4	1–4	No. of sample trees	0	1	2	3+4	2–4	1–4
Austria								52592	76.6	20.9	2.1	0.4	2.5	23.4
Belgium–Flanders	535	74.6	18.0	4.7	1.9	6.6	24.6	1	100.0	0.0	0.0	0.0	0.0	0.0
Belgium–Wallonia	80	38.8	42.5	18.7	0.0	18.7	61.2	553	52.6	34.6	10.8	2.0	12.8	47.4
Bulgaria	378	18.0	43.0	32.0	7.0	39.0	82.0	80	45.4	53.4	1.2	0.0	1.2	54.6
Czechoslovakia	178	81.0	12.0	5.0	2.0	7.0	19.0	7986	30.7	45.5	19.5	4.3	23.8	69.3
Denmark	178	81.0	12.0	5.0	2.0	7.0	19.0	911	24.9	30.9	37.5	6.7	44.2	75.1
Denmark	535	74.2	17.6	8.0	0.2	8.2	25.8	911	24.9	30.9	37.5	6.7	44.2	75.1
Finland	289	92.7	5.6	1.7	0.0	1.7	7.3	123	77.2	16.3	5.7	0.8	6.5	22.8
France									59.1	27.8	10.4	2.7	13.1	40.9
German Dem.Rep.*	20070	71.9	22.7	5.1	0.3	5.4	28.1							
Germany, Fed.Rep.	31798							19874	17.8	53.2	27.9	1.1	29.0	82.2
Greece	199	89.9	4.6	1.0	4.5	5.5	10.1	23	82.6	4.4	0.0	13.0	13.0	17.4
Hungary														
Ireland***	298	85.7	14.3	0.0	0.0	0.0	14.3	4349	80.2	14.6	4.6	0.6	5.2	19.8
Italy–Bolzano									53.0					
Italy–Tuscany									27.6	40.3	29.5	2.6	32.1	72.4
Liechtenstein*	1141	79.0	15.9	3.9	1.2	5.1	21.0	370	70.4	24.0	4.8	0.8	5.6	29.6
Luxembourg	2550	50.8	31.0	15.1	3.1	18.2	49.2	125	24.5	40.4	27.1	8.0	35.1	75.5
Netherlands	936	88.5	8.0	3.3	0.2	3.5	11.5	1235	40.9	30.1	25.0	4.0	29.0	59.1
Norway	5863	50.8	27.4	18.1	3.7	21.8	49.2	13346	30.7	41.1	25.5	2.7	28.2	69.3
Poland														
Portugal														
Spain	1707	84.0	13.7	2.1	0.2	2.3	16.0	3642	53.0	32.0	13.0	2.0	15.0	47.0
Sweden								3462	77.0	20.0	3.0	0.0	3.0	23.0
Switzerland*														
Turkey														
United Kingdom**	533	35.0	34.0	24.0	7.0	31.0	65.0							
USSR–Estonia														
USSR–Lithuania	5888	87.0	12.0	1.0	0.0	1.0	13.0							
Yugoslavia														

sources: country reports

* all ages
** data refer to Picea sitchensis
*** data refer to 235 Picea sitchensis and 63 Picea abies

Table 7. Defoliation in **pine** (by age groups; by classes and aggregates).

Countries	No. of sample trees	percent trees defoliated, up to 60 years old						No. of sample trees	percent trees defoliated, >60 years old					
		0	1	2	3+4	2−4	1−4		0	1	2	3+4	2−4	1−4
Austria	395	55.4	37.7	6.1	0.8	6.9	44.6	10302	57.9	38.3	2.9	0.9	3.8	42.1
Belgium–Flanders	29	58.6	27.6	13.8	0.0	13.8	41.4	38	47.4	42.1	7.9	2.6	10.5	52.6
Belgium–Wallonia	1080	37.2	55.6	6.9	0.3	7.2	62.8	57	80.7	8.7	7.0	3.6	10.6	19.3
Bulgaria	119	3.0	17.0	54.0	26.0	80.0	97.0	160	75.0	25.0	0.0	0.0	0.0	25.0
Czechoslovakia								924	23.4	28.0	27.5	11.1	38.6	66.6
Denmark														
Finland	1110	82.3	14.4	3.1	0.2	3.3	17.7	1048	61.4	26.4	11.2	1.0	12.2	38.6
France	232	66.4	25.0	7.3	1.3	8.6	33.6	232	47.0	34.4	15.5	3.1	18.6	53.0
German Dem.Rep. *	47340	58.2	33.3	7.9	0.6	8.5	41.8		48.4	35.1	13.4	3.1	16.5	51.6
Germany, Fed.Rep.	14177	40.8	53.1	6.1	0.0	6.1	59.2	12189	33.5	51.2	13.7	1.6	15.3	66.5
Greece ****	1385	71.2	18.4	8.8	1.6	10.4	28.8	116	43.1	49.1	7.8	0.0	7.8	56.9
Hungary	164	62.8	29.9	6.7	0.6	7.3	37.2	101	89.1	8.9	2.0	1.0	3.0	11.9
Ireland **	346	32.1	28.9	37.0	2.0	39.0	67.9							
Italy–Bolzano *								782	76.9	16.2	5.7	1.2	6.9	23.1
Italy–Tuscany***								117	20.5	43.6	32.5	3.4	35.9	79.5
Liechtenstein *									39.0					61.0
Luxembourg														
Netherlands	19975	77.4	17.1	4.6	0.9	5.5	22.6	9450	66.4	24.0	7.6	2.0	9.6	33.6
Norway	397	85.4	11.3	3.0	0.3	3.3	14.6	914	28.6	44.6	22.5	4.3	26.8	71.4
Poland	144210	43.9	33.4	19.1	3.6	22.7	56.1	124088	39.5	34.8	21.5	4.2	25.7	60.5
Portugal	1907	93.6	4.6	1.6	0.2	1.8	6.4	51	100.0	0.0	0.0	0.0	0.0	0.0
Spain	3509	71.0	21.5	6.5	1.0	7.5	29.0	685	70.1	23.4	5.5	1.0	6.5	29.9
Sweden	1301	87.4	10.8	1.5	0.3	1.8	12.6	3743	48.6	42.5	7.8	1.1	8.9	51.4
Switzerland *								380	37.0	41.0	16.0	6.0	22.0	63.0
Turkey	198	20.0	47.0	27.0	6.0	33.0	80.0							
United Kingdom														
USSR–Estonia														
USSR–Lithuania	10160	75.0	21.0	3.0	1.0	4.0	25.0							
Yugoslavia									63.0	32.0	5.0	0.0	5.0	37.0

sources: country reports
* all ages
** data refer to *Pinus contorta*
*** data refer to *Pinus pinea*
**** data refer to *Pinus nigra*

Table 8. Defoliation in **fir** (by age groups; by classes and aggregates).

Countries	No. of sample trees	percent trees defoliated, up to 60 years old						No. of sample trees	percent trees defoliated, >60 years old					
		0	1	2	3+4	2–4	1–4		0	1	2	3+4	2–4	1–4
Austria								2614	41.0	39.9	15.8	3.3	19.1	59.0
Belgium–Flanders														
Belgium–Wallonia														
Bulgaria	80	45.0	35.5	20.5	0.0	20.5	56.0	40	49.5	47.8	2.7	0.0	2.7	50.5
Czechoslovakia														
Denmark														
Finland														
France	97	77.3	14.5	8.2	0.0	8.2	22.7	186	38.2	34.9	24.2	2.7	26.9	61.8
German Dem.Rep.														
Germany, Fed.Rep.	1059	67.3	23.8	7.6	2.3	9.9	33.7	2220	49.0	31.1	57.3	6.7	64.0	95.1
Greece **	27	7.4	33.3	44.4	14.8	59.2	92.5.	241	48.1	40.3	10.0	1.6	11.6	51.9
Hungary														
Ireland														
Italy–Bolzano	333	78.1	18.3	3.6	0.0	3.6	21.9	138	79.8	14.4	5.8	0.0	5.8	20.2
Italy–Tuscany								134	29.8	31.3	30.7	8.2	38.9	70.2
Liechtenstein									25.0					75.0
Luxembourg														
Netherlands														
Norway														
Poland	1920	61.8	22.9	12.9	2.4	15.3	38.2	4724	44.0	29.5	22.0	4.5	26.5	56.0
Portugal														
Spain														
Sweden														
Switzerland*								913	51.0	35.0	11.0	3.0	14.0	49.0
Turkey														
United Kingdom														
USSR–Estonia														
USSR–Lithuania														
Yugoslavia														

sources: country reports

* all ages

** data refer to *Abies cephalonica*

Table 9. Defoliation in **beech** (by age groups; by classes and aggregates).

Countries	No. of sample trees	percent trees defoliated, up to 60 years old						No. of sample trees	percent trees defoliated, >60 years old					
		0	1	2	3+4	2–4	1–4		0	1	2	3+4	2–4	1–4
Austria	8	62.5	25.0	12.5	0.0	12.5	37.5							
Belgium–Flanders								2251	52.9	40.9	5.5	0.7	6.2	47.1
Belgium–Wallonia								35	60.0	31.4	5.7	2.9	8.6	40.0
Bulgaria	560	85.0	14.3	0.7	0.0	0.7	15.0							
Czechoslovakia	441	30.0	41.0	25.0	4.0	29.0	70.0	400	72.7	23.7	3.0	0.6	3.6	27.3
Denmark	34	12.0	74.0	14.0	0.0	14.0	88.0	905	37.0	44.0	17.0	2.0	19.0	63.0
Finland								63	0.0	84.0	16.0	0.0	16.0	100.0
France	130	86.9	8.5	3.8	0.8	4.6	13.1	289	79.6	17.3	3.1	0.0	3.1	20.4
German Dem.Rep. *	6750								75.1	21.1	3.4	0.4	3.8	24.9
Germany, Fed.Rep.	7552	60.5	32.3	6.9	0.3	7.2	39.5	14972	24.3	54.5	20.6	0.6	21.2	75.7
Greece								53	0.0	49.1	49.0	1.9	50.9	100.0
Hungary	552	90.2	8.2	1.4	0.2	1.6	9.8	727	89.7	9.1	1.0	0.2	1.2	10.3
Ireland														
Italy–Bolzano														
Italy–Tuscany	1640	41.2	38.9	18.6	1.3	19.9	58.8	201	47.8	41.3	10.4	0.5	10.9	52.2
Liechtenstein														
Luxembourg	114	72.0	22.8	5.2	0.0	5.2	28.0	1351	49.9	41.6	8.5	0.0	8.5	50.1
Netherlands	1275	35.8	46.6	15.3	2.3	17.6	64.2	1200	30.8	42.6	23.2	3.4	26.6	69.2
Norway														
Poland	4488	89.8	6.2	2.1	1.9	4.0	10.2	12474	91.5	5.6	1.6	1.3	2.9	8.5
Portugal														
Spain	44	97.7	2.3	0.0	0.0	0.0	2.3							
Sweden								140	87.1	10.7	1.4	0.8	2.2	12.9
Switzerland*								2399	84.6	12.0	3.2	0.2	3.4	15.4
Turkey								1524	65.0	28.0	6.0	1.0	7.0	35.0
United Kingdom														
USSR–Estonia	17	59.0	24.0	12.0	5.0	17.0	41.0	19	26.0	63.0	11.0	0.0	11.0	74.0
USSR–Lithuania														
Yugoslavia														

sources: country reports

* all ages

Table 10. Defoliation in **oak** (by age groups; by classes and aggregates).

Countries	percent trees defoliated, up to 60 years old							percent trees defoliated, >60 years old						
	No. of sample trees	0	1	2	3+4	2–4	1–4	No. of sample trees	0	1	2	3+4	2–4	1–4
Austria								550	35.7	46.6	14.7	3.0	17.7	64.3
Belgium–Flanders	42	47.6	50.0	2.4	0.0	2.4	52.4	155	31.0	46.4	18.1	4.5	22.6	69.0
Belgium–Wallonia														
Bulgaria	600	48.8	34.4	12.3	4.5	16.8	51.2	176	15.0	45.0	30.0	10.0	40.0	85.0
Czechoslovakia	316	17.0	38.0	33.0	12.0	45.0	83.0							
Denmark														
Finland	223	83.4	15.7	0.9	0.0	0.9	16.6	351	76.6	19.7	3.7	0.0	3.7	23.4
France	3960	52.2	37.6	9.7	0.5	10.2	47.8		57.4	27.6	11.4	3.6	15.0	42.6
German Dem.Rep.*	3445	20.7	50.9	27.4	1.0	28.4	79.3	7817	20.6	49.4	28.7	1.3	30.0	79.4
Germany, Fed.Rep.	285	79.2	13.5	2.9	4.4	7.3	20.8	15	0.0	60.0	33.3	6.7	40.0	100.0
Greece***								941	66.2	20.9	6.5	6.4	12.9	33.8
Hungary	2724	53.4	33.2	11.8	1.6	13.4	46.6							
Ireland														
Italy–Bolzano	1268	66.3	33.7	0.0	0.0	0.0	33.7	294	39.2	35.0	25.5	0.3	25.8	60.8
Italy–Tuscany**														
Liechtenstein	86	25.5	42.3	25.6	6.6	32.2	74.5	693	30.5	55.1	14.4	0.0	14.4	69.5
Luxembourg														
Netherlands	7675	72.8	18.6	6.7	1.9	8.6	27.2	3250	13.4	38.0	37.0	11.6	48.6	86.6
Norway	8422	97.3	2.7	0.0	0.0	0.0	2.7	11501	69.8	19.7	8.3	2.2	10.5	30.2
Poland	516	52.8	39.6	7.3	0.3	7.6	47.2	670	99.2	0.8	0.0	0.0	0.0	0.8
Portugal**								1105	66.2	26.9	6.0	0.9	6.9	33.8
Spain*	1155	32.0	43.0	25.0	0.0	25.0	68.0	1201	62.7	28.5	8.6	0.2	8.8	37.3
Sweden														
Switzerland								127	56.0	37.0	6.0	1.0	7.0	44.0
Turkey														
United Kingdom	28							55	4.0	33.0	55.0	8.0	63.0	96.0
USSR–Estonia									75.0	21.0	4.0	0.0	4.0	25.0
USSR–Lithuania	346	94.	06.0	0.0	0.0	0.0	6.0							
Yugoslavia														

sources: country reports
* all ages
** data refer to *Quercus ilex*
*** data refer to *Quercus frainetto*

Table 11. Intensity of defoliation in **all species**, based on national and regional surveys.*

Country	Defoliation (percent trees affected)		
	none class 0	slight class 1	moderate to severe classes 2-4
Portugal	96.5	2.2	1.3
USSR–Lithuania	79.0	18.0	3.0
Austria	71.2	25.2	3.6
Italy–Bolzano	79.8	15.0	5.2
France	77.3	15.8	6.9
Spain	68.6	24.4	7.0
Hungary	78.5	14.0	7.5
Bulgaria	57.0	34.9	8.1
Yugoslavia	67.6	22.4	10.0
Luxembourg	57.6	32.1	10.3
Belgium–Flanders	53.8	35.8	10.4
Sweden	61.3	28.1	10.6
Switzerland	57.0	31.0	12.0
German Dem. Rep.	55.6	30.6	13.8
Germany, Fed.Rep.of	47.6	37.5	14.9
Finland	61.2	22.7	16.1
Greece	36.0	47.0	17.0
Liechtenstein	50.0	33.0	17.0
Denmark	51.0	31.0	18.0
Netherlands	52.4	29.3	18.3
Italy–Tuscany	48.9	32.4	18.7
Poland	50.6	29.0	20.4
United Kingdom	36.0	39.0	25.0
Czechoslovakia	29.5	43.1	27.4

* Comparisons between countries should be made with caution

Table 12. Intensity of defoliation in **conifers**, based on national and regional surveys.*

Country	Defoliation (percent trees affected)		
	none class 0	slight class 1	moderate to severe classes 2-4
Portugal	94.0	4.3	1.7
USSR–Lithuania	75.0	22.0	3.0
Austria	72.4	24.3	3.3
Ireland	69.9	25.3	4.8
Italy–Bolzano	79.6	15.2	5.2
Spain	70.8	21.9	7.3
Bulgaria	53.8	38.5	7.7
Greece	49.0	43.3	7.7
USSR–Estonia	48.0	43.0	9.0
France	72.7	18.2	9.1
Hungary	74.0	16.6	9.4
Belgium–Flanders	53.3	35.9	10.8
Belgium–Wallonia	65.0	24.0	11.0
Luxembourg	68.1	20.8	11.1
Sweden	55.8	31.9	12.3
Germany, Fed.Rep.of	50.6	35.4	14.0
Netherlands	60.9	24.6	14.5
Switzerland	52.0	33.0	15.0
Italy–Tuscany	63.6	21.0	15.4
German Dem. Rep.	51.4	33.1	15.5
Finland*	60.5	22.5	17.0
Yugoslavia	54.5	28.0	17.5
Norway	49.7	29.5	20.8
Denmark	65.0	14.0	21.0
Liechtenstein	42.0	35.0	23.0
Poland	42.4	33.4	24.2
United Kingdom	33.0	40.0	27.0
Czechoslovakia	29.0	44.0	27.0

* Comparisons between countries should be made with caution

Table 13. Intensity of defoliation in **broadleaves**, based on national and regional surveys.*

Country	Defoliation (percent trees affected)		
	none class 0	slight class 1	moderate to severe classes 2-4
Portugal	93.9	5.3	0.8
USSR–Lithuania	90.0	9.0	1.0
Italy–Bolzano	88.5	8.6	2.9
Liechtenstein	68.0	27.0	5.0
Sweden	77.3	17.5	5.2
France	80.2	14.5	5.3
Spain	66.2	27.0	6.8
Bulgaria	65.9	27.3	6.8
Hungary	79.4	13.6	7.0
Switzerland	67.0	26.0	7.0
Poland	79.5	13.4	7.1
Finland	67.6	24.5	7.9
Austria	51.7	40.3	8.0
German Dem. Rep.	66.9	24.1	9.0
Yugoslavia	69.7	21.3	9.0
Belgium–Flanders	54.3	35.7	10.0
Luxembourg	51.2	36.5	12.3
Denmark	30.0	56.0	14.0
Germany, Fed.Rep.of	41.5	42.0	16.5
United Kingdom	41.0	39.0	20.0
Italy–Tuscany	43.9	36.0	20.1
Netherlands	36.9	37.7	25.4
Greece	19.8	51.7	28.5
Czechoslovakia	31.5	39.4	29.1

* Comparisons between countries should be made with caution

Table 14. Comparison of forest damage survey results from 1986, 1987 and 1988, for **coniferous** and **broadleaved** species (all ages).

Country	conifers				broadleaves			
	Defoliation classes 2-4			% change	Defoliation classes 2-4			% change
	1986	1987	1988	±	1986	1987	1988	±
Austria	4.5	3.5	3.3	-0.2	5.5	7.8	8.0	+0.2
Belgium – Flanders	–	4.7	10.8	+6.1	–	16.0	10.0	-6.0
Bulgaria	4.7	3.8	7.7	+3.9	4.0	3.1	6.8	+3.7
Czechoslovakia	16.4	15.6	27.0	+11.4	not assessed	20.0	14.0	-6.0
Denmark	–	24.0	21.0	-3.0	–	4.7	7.9	+3.2
Finland	–	13.5	17.0	+3.5	4.8	6.5	5.3	-1.2
France	12.5	12.0	9.1	-2.9	16.8	19.2	16.5	-2.7
Germany, Federal Republic of	19.5	15.9	14.0	-1.9	–	3.6	2.9	-0.7
Italy – Bolzano	–	3.1	5.2	+2.1	–	7.0	5.0	-2.0
Liechtenstein	22.0	27.0	23.0	-4.0	10.0	10.1	12.3	+2.2
Luxembourg	4.2	3.8	11.1	+7.3	5.6	26.5	25.4	-1.1
Netherlands	28.9	18.7	14.5	-4.2	13.2	13.7	6.8	-6.9
Spain	18.2	10.7	7.3	-3.4	not assessed		5.2	
Sweden	11.1	5.6	12.3	+6.7	8.0	15.0	7.0	-8.0
Switzerland	16.0	14.0	15.0	+1.0	–	20.0	20.0	0.0
United Kingdom	–	23.0	27.0	+4.0	–	7.3	9.0	+1.7
Yugoslavia*	23.0	16.1	17.5	+1.4	not assessed		1.0	
USSR – Lithuania	–	14.8	3.0	-11.8	not assessed			

* regional survey in 1988

Part THREE

EFFECTS OF MERCURY RELATED TO

LONG-RANGE ATMOSPHERIC TRANSPORT

Mercury as an environmental pollutant has been documented in numerous investigations during past decades. Already in the mid 1950s mercury showed evidence of its highly toxic character to humans in Minamata (Japan) where many people were seriously injured or died as a result of eating fish from waters contaminated by mercury pollution. Since then, mercury pollution has been reported in a large number of waters all over the world. Often it has been possible to trace the sources to single outlets of mercury from various industries (Förstner and Wittmann 1981).

More recently, however, a new pattern of mercury pollution has been discerned, mostly in Scandinavia and North America. Fish from low productive lakes even in remote areas have also been found to have high mercury contents. This pollution problem cannot be connected to single mercury discharges but is owing to more widespread air-pollution and the long-range transport of pollutants. A large number of waters are affected and the problem has a regional dimension (Wren and MacCrimmon, 1983; Björklund et al., 1984; Hakanson et al., 1988). Our awareness of mercury contamination of the environment has evolved from a situation of "localized and acute" problems owing to point-source discharges (1950s to 1970s) to a more recent situation that may be characterized as "regional and chronic" problems owing to diffuse sources (Sheffy, 1987).

I. THE MERCURY PROBLEM

In Sweden the content of mercury in fish from lakes not affected by local sources has been compiled in several reports (Björklund et al., 1984; Lindqvist et al., 1984; Hakanson et al., 1988). The content in northern pike (Esox lucius) has been used as an indicator organism. The regional surveys have shown that the mercury content is generally and substantially increased in the southern and central parts of the country. Here, regional mean values were found in the range 0.5 to 1.2 mg/kg in pike (figure 1).

In about 10,000 lakes in Sweden, the mercury content in pike exceeded the blacklisting limit, according to estimations from the regional surveys (Hakanson et al., 1988). In Sweden, a limit of 1 mg/kg in 1 kg pike is used. Fish from blacklisted lakes may not be sold or given away and it is recommended that fish from these lakes should not be consumed by humans.

Internationally, limits for mercury in fish are mostly established in the 0.4 to 1.0 mg/kg range. The national limits are often complemented by dietary recommendations. In particular, pregnant women should be cautious about consuming fish containing mercury. During early stages of development the foetus is very sensitive to exposure to methyl mercury. Elevated intakes of mercury via fish during pregnancy may result in a delay in the development of the child (Kjellström et al., 1986). Human exposure to methyl mercury is almost entirely by way of consumption of fish and seafood (Nordberg et al., 1985).

The natural background contents of mercury in fish have been estimated to have been 0.05 to 0.2 (National Institute for Public Health, 1970), 0.02 to 0.2 (Huckabee et al., 1974), about 0.2 (Lindqvist et al., 1984) or 0.15 mg/kg (Hakanson, 1984). Verta et al. (1986) discussed the natural Hg content in fish in relation to the content of humic matter in the waters. According to this study, the most probable natural content has been 0.05 to 0.3 mg/kg regarding colour values in the waters in the range 0 to 100 mg Pt/l. Obviously, the content of mercury was markedly increased in a large part of Sweden by a factor of about 4 to 6. Only in the most northern part of the country was the content in fish close to natural values (Björklund et al., 1984). Even though mercury emissions in Sweden have been drastically curtailed since the late 1960s, no apparent decrease in the mercury content of fish from forest lakes has been observed. On the contrary, trend analysis indicates that the mercury content in 1 kg pike seems to increase with time (Hakanson et al., 1988).

In Finland also, the mercury content in fish has generally increased. In 67 lakes, classified as forest lakes (forest and peatland representing 80 per cent or more of the catchment area and no large municipalities) the mean 1 kg pike content was 0.56 mg/kg. A clear regional difference was found between Hg content in pike in southern and central Finland, on the one hand, and northern Finland, on the other. A lower level, 0.28, was recorded in the north (Verta *et al.*, 1986). The mercury level in pike in southern and central Finland was estimated to have increased during the past 100 years by a factor of about two. The most probable reason for this was concluded to be an increased load of atmospheric mercury (Verta *et al.*, 1986).

In Canada, especially in the Precambrian Shield region, fish show elevated levels of mercury also in lakes remote from any direct source of contamination (Brouzes *et al.*, 1977; Wren *et al.*, 1983). Many of the lakes in Ontario contain fish, especially the larger and older specimens, which have a mercury concentration in excess of 1.5 ppm in their soft tissue (Evans 1986). Studies of 14 precambrian lakes in Ontario suggested that acid stress and terrestrial imports of mercury enhanced mercury uptake in fish (Suns *et al.*, 1980).

In the United States of America, elevated contents of mercury in fish due to air pollution have been reported from some areas. Akielaszek and Haines (1981) found that elevated levels were characteristic of certain species in northern Maine. This was probably a result of a combination of factors, including trophic status of the fish, increased uptake of mercury by fish under oligotrophic conditions and some source of mercury input into these aquatic systems. In the Lake Superior region, Glass *et al.* (1986) reported that atmospheric deposition was probably the major source of mercury in some lakes, resulting in high residue levels in the aquatic biota.

In the State of Wisconsin, the mercury limits set by the United States Food and Drug Administration are exceeded in approximately 90 water bodies out of about 300 tested. Consumption of mercury-contaminated fish poses a potential health risk to the citizens of Wisconsin (Sheffy, 1987). A potentially significant fraction of the mercury burden in fish in the north-central Wisconsin lakes is implied to be of atmospheric origin (Rada *et al.*, 1989).

The mercury content in fish tissue is almost entirely in the form of monomethyl mercury (Huckabee *et al.*, 1979). Methyl mercury is produced in soil, water and sediment, mainly by microbiological processes. Biologically this form of mercury is highly active and accumulating in the trophic chain.

II. CAUSES

The increase of mercury in fish in lakes is mainly attributable to two factors: a general increase in the transport of mercury to the lakes and the acidification of lake waters (Hakanson, 1975; Björklund *et al.*, 1984; Lindqvist *et al.*, 1984; Hakanson *et al.*, 1988).

A. Increased load

Analyses of mercury in sediment from Swedish forest lakes showed clearly that the transport of mercury to lakes had increased sharply during the twentieth century in the southern and central parts of Sweden. The increase could hardly be due to natural factors, but must have had anthropogenic causes (Lindqvist *et al.*, 1984; Johansson, 1985). In the southern and central parts of Sweden, the content of mercury in the top layers of the sediment showed, on average, about five times higher values than the background levels. In the most northern part of Sweden, only minor increments in the top layers of sediment have been recorded, indicating that the mercury load in the lakes in this region does not seem to have increased greatly - at most by a factor of two. In a broad outline, the regional concentrations of mercury in fish and top sediment show a similar pattern (Lindqvist *et al.*, 1984; Johansson, 1985).

Hakanson *et al.* (1988) studied the correlation between the mercury content in pike and geographical, physical and chemical parameters from a broad set of data from 1,456 lakes. The highest correlation was found to mercury content in sediment ($r = 0.66$). This also indicates a marked impact on an increased load on the present mercury concentrations in fish. It is reasonable to assume that the increased mercury load causes a general increase of the mercury content in pike from the probable natural background levels of about 0.05 to 0.3 mg/kg to a basic level of about 0.5 to 0.9 mg/kg in lakes in southern and central Sweden. This basic level is the average value for non-acidified lakes in different regions. About 40,000 out of about 83,000 lakes larger than 0.01 km^2 in Sweden have been estimated to be affected by these increments (Lindqvist *et al.*, 1984).

An increased load of mercury in remote lakes has also been reported from other parts of Scandinavia and North America. In southern Finland, a distinct increase in mercury concentration was observed in recent lake sediment. In northern Finland only a slight or zero increase was recorded. The increase in the southern part of the country was concluded to be mainly a result of increased atmospheric deposition (Rekolainen *et al.*, 1986; Tolonen and Jaakola, 1983). The most remarkable increase of mercury in the lakes started in the years 1920 to 1930 (Rekolainen *et al.*, 1986) or in the early 1950s (Tolonen and Jaakola, 1983).

Studies of sediment from remote lakes in south-central Ontario (Canada) (Evans, 1986; Johnson *et al.*, 1986), have shown a general decrease with sediment depth, indicating a substantial increase in mercury loading in lakes in recent decades. The major source of the mercury in the lakes studied was atmospheric deposition of material originating from outside the catchments (Evans, 1986). In lakes in Quebec in eastern Canada, Quellet and Jones (1983) recorded significantly increased levels of mercury in sediment from 1940 onwards. It was suggested that the major sources of heavy metal deposition, including mercury, in the province of Quebec were the heavily industrialized American midwest and the Great Lakes regions.

In the north-eastern part of the United States of America, enhancement of mercury in top sediment layers has been reported from lakes in northern Maine (Akielaszek and Haines, 1981), the Adirondacks region, New York State (Heit *et al.*) and in the north-central part of Wisconsin (Rada *et al.*, 1989).

B. Acidification of lakes

In many studies, a correlation between mercury content in fish and pH has been demonstrated. In lakes with low pH values, the mercury content in fish is generally higher than in less acidic lakes (e.g. Brouzes *et al.*, 1977; Suns *et al.*, 1980; Björklund *et al.*, 1984; Wren and MacCrimmon, 1983; Hakanson *et al.*, 1988). When a lake is acidified, changes occur in the turnover of substances and in the biotic structure of the ecosystem of the lake that indirectly affects the flow and turnover of mercury. Many processes have been proposed to explain the increased mercury content in fish in acidic lakes, for example:

(a) Decreased productivity in acidic lakes favours higher bio-accumulation in the aquatic ecosystem (Huckabee *et al.*, 1979; Lindqvist *et al.*, 1984);

(b) A successively changed composition of the fish population by the acidification results in a higher uptake of mercury in the top predator fish community (Björklund *et al.*, 1984);

(c) An increased net rate of methyl mercury production in waters and sediment in acid lakes (Xun *et al.*, 1987);

(d) The activity of mercury in natural waters is essentially regulated by the activity of S^{2-} which in turn is strongly affected by pH conditions (Björnberg *et al.*, 1988).

In addition to the generally increased level of mercury in fish owing to an increased load, the acidification of lakes has caused a further increase of mercury content in fish in about 10,000 lakes in Sweden. In these lakes the mercury content in pike has probably risen further by about 0.1 to 0.3 mg/kg and in some cases even by 1 mg/kg in addition to the already elevated basic level (Lindqvist *et al.*, 1988).

Restriction on emissions of both mercury and acidifying substances is strongly needed in order to reduce the mercury content in literally thousands of lakes. Reduced acidification of waters would lower the mercury content in fish in many of the acidified lakes, but to obtain a more general effect, the atmospheric deposition of mercury must be reduced.

III. MERCURY IN AIR AND ATMOSPHERIC DEPOSITION

A. Sources of mercury

On a global scale, the sources of mercury emissions to the atmosphere can be considered as being of continental or oceanic origin. The interhemispheric distribution of mercury in air over oceanic areas shows a concentration in the northern hemisphere twice the level in the southern hemisphere. This pattern supports the assumption that terrestrial sources are more important than oceanic. However, the oceanic input could still be quite significant in the global perspective (Slemr *et al.*, 1981; Fitzgerald, 1986).

The relative importance of human-related activities is most certainly quite large. The human-related emissions in Europe and Sweden in the late 1970s, for example, have been estimated to constitute 90 and 50 per cent of the total emissions in these areas, respectively (Lindqvist and Rodhe, 1985). Fossil fuel combustion for power generation, outlets from chlor-alkali plants and waste incineration are important sources of mercury emissions to the atmosphere. About 25 per cent of mercury emissions to the atmosphere are estimated to be the result of electric power production (Lindqvist, 1986). Waste incineration was estimated to constitute about 50 per cent of total mercury emissions to the atmosphere in Sweden in 1984 (Johansson *et al.*, 1988). Today, yearly emissions from waste incineration are estimated to be about 1 tonne of mercury compared to 3 tonnes 1984.

B. Mercury in air

Mercury concentrations in air are normally in the range 1 to 4 ng Hg m^{-3}. A mercury level of 1 ng m^{-3} is generally present in air over oceanic areas in the southern hemisphere, while the corresponding figure for the northern hemisphere is about 2 ng m^{-3} (Fitzgerald, 1986).

In the late 1970s and early 1980s, measurements of mercury in air at coastal sites as well as over continental regions representing "clean air" areas (that is, no influence of local sources) have given values of about 2 to 4 ng Hg m^{-3} (Brosset,·1982; Ferrara, 1982; Fitzgerald *et al.*, 1983). More recent measurements in Sweden in the period 1983 to 1984 (Brosset, 1987) and the Nordic countries in 1985 to 1987 (Iverfeldt and Roche, 1988) have confirmed these values. Generally, the mercury levels in air increase during the winter period (3-4 ng m^{-3}) compared to the summer (1.5-3 ng m^{-3}). Further, elevated concentrations in air over Scandinavia are found in the southern wind-sectors (Brosset, 1982; Iverfeldt and Rodhe, 1988).

The atmospheric particulate mercury concentration is normally less than 0.1 ng Hg m^{-3} (Fitzgerald, 1986; Iverfeldt and Rodhe, 1988; Brosset and Iverfeldt, 1989) or even at the sub-picogram per cubic metre level in remote open ocean areas of the southern hemisphere.

C. Mercury in precipitation

Mercury levels in precipitation are generally in the range 1 to 100 ng Hg L^{-1} (reviewed in Lindqvist and Rodhe, 1985), with baseline mercury concentrations at about 1 to 25 ng L^{-1} (Drabaek and Iverfeldt, 1988). In industrial areas, considerably higher levels can sometimes be found. Ahmed *et al.* (1987) have reported values up to 1,140 ng Hg L^{-1} in rain water collected in industrial regions of the Federal Republic of Germany and levels up to 80 ng Hg L^{-1}

in rain from relatively unpolluted areas. Recent data on mercury concentrations in rain in the Nordic countries show yearly mean levels at about 20 to 40 ng Hg L^{-1} in the southern and central parts. In the north, yearly mean values at about 10 ng Hg L^{-1} are more representative (Iverfeldt and Rodhe, 1988; Iverfeldt (publication in preparation)).

D. Different forms of mercury

The elemental mercury from Hg° seems to constitute 95 to 100 per cent of the total mercury concentration in air (Bloom and Fitzerland, 1988). Previously, Lindqvist and Rodhe (1985) considered the relative amount of elemental mercury to be less than or equal to 80 per cent of the total gaseous mercury.

Various mercury forms behave in different ways in the atmosphere. For example, Lindqvist and Rodhe (1985) estimated the atmospheric residence time for elemental mercury to be somewhere between a few months up to two years. The residence time of the remaining non-elemental part of the total gaseous mercury is probably in the range extending from a few days to a few weeks. In a study from Long Island Sound (USA), Bloom and Fitzgerald (1988) reported monomethyl mercury levels between 0 and 5 per cent of the total mercury content in air, the rest being elemental mercury.

Mercury in precipitation can be divided into different chemical forms. In a Swedish study, Brosset (1987) found a minor mercury form to be relatively constant, that is independent of when and where the rain was collected. A major form, probably associated with anthropogenic activities, was found to be dependent on sampling location and the transport direction. This mercury form is also present in smoke from coal-fired power plants (Brosset, 1983, 1987) and is probably transported over long distances with air masses and, subsequently scavenged by cloud or rain droplets.

The part of the gaseous mercury in air over Sweden that is dependent on transport direction is related to the soot concentration in the air (Brosset, 1982). This correlation between mercury in air and receptor-oriented trajectories and soot demonstrates the existence of long-range transport from the European continent to Sweden. In a similar way, long-range transport has been associated with high deposition of Hg in remote areas in the United States of America (Glass *et al.* 1986).

E. Deposition of mercury

A decreasing south-north gradient of atmospheric mercury concentrations exists across Sweden (Brosset, 1987) and indeed across the Nordic countries (Iverfeldt and Rodhe, 1988). The gradient is more pronounced in precipitation than in air. Analysis of back trajectories and a correlation between mercury and sulphate concentrations in rain water indicates that European continental sources are responsible for a major part of the mercury deposited by precipitation in the Nordic countries (Iverfeldt and Rodhe, 1988). A comparison of data from a primary study of a peat bog in northern Sweden (Jensen, 1988) with data from a peat bog in Denmark (Pheiffer Madsen, 1981) shows a considerably lower deposition value at the former location, of 5 to about 50 μg m^{-2} yr^{-1}.

Fitzgerald (1986) estimated the range of annual depositional fluxes to be between 4 and about 40 μg m^{-2} yr^{-1}, going from remote open ocean areas to areas with greater anthropogenic impact. This range compares well with the deposition rates calculated from a new precipitation data set collected in the Nordic countries from 1985 to 1988 (Iverfeldt (in preparation)). In Sweden, moss analyses (*Hylocomium splendens*) have been used to study the deposition pattern of mercury (Rühling *et al.* (in preparation)). The preliminary results from this qualitative study support the assumption that long-range transport from the European continent is responsible for a large mercury deposition on southern and central Sweden.

IV. TRANSPORT OF MERCURY IN SOIL AND WATER IN FOREST AREAS

The processes and transportation of mercury from forest soils into water and into the aquatic organisms are closely related to the flow of organic matter. In both the terrestrial and the aquatic environments, mercury is strongly associated with humic substances (Strohal and Huljev, 1971; Hakanson, 1974; Benes *et al.*, 1976; Andersson, 1979; Schnitzer and Kerndorf, 1981; Rae and Aston, 1982; Lodenius *et al.*, 1983). Unlike the case of most other metals, acidification of soil and water does not increase the solubility of mercury. Absorption on humic matter seems instead to increase at lower pH values (Hakanson, 1974; Jackson *et al.*, 1980; Schindler *et al.*, 1980; Lodenius *et al.*, 1983; Lodenius, 1987).

Atmospheric mercury deposited onto podzolic soils - the most common type of forest soil in Sweden - is effectively retained in the humic-rich upper parts of the forest soil (Andersson, 1979; Ek, 1986). It is probable that the vertical transport down to deeper soil levels is of minor importance. This is supported by the fact that deeper ground-water levels, with low content of humic matter, have very low concentrations of mercury, less than 1 ng/l (Aastrup, 1986).

Mercury is transported from the soils to watercourses and lakes mainly during periods of high ground-water level in the soils and high run-off amounts. These periods are characterized by high concentrations of mercury and humic matter in the waters. The specific transport of mercury has been measured to be 0.7 to 6.1 g/km^2 per year in small watersheds in southern and central Sweden and 1.2 to 1.8 in areas in the northern part of the country (Iverfeldt and Johansson, 1988).

About 25 to 75 per cent of the total load of mercury in lakes in southern and central Sweden originates from run-off from the catchment area. In lakes where the total load is high, transport from run-off is the dominant pathway (Iverfeldt and Johnsson, 1988). Hence, the concentrations of mercury in the upper part of the forest soil are an important factor determining the load of mercury in lakes. The present load of atmospheric mercury on the surface of lakes in southern and central Finland is only about one third of the amount of mercury that is annually sedimented to the bottom. The mercury leached from the catchment area represents the main load of mercury on a typical small forest lake in southern Finland. This conclusion is consistent with findings of good correlations between mercury in pike and morphometric variables (Verta *et al.*, 1986). Björklund and Norling (1979), Suns *et al.* (1980) and Verta *et al.* (1986) have found strong correlations between mercury in fish and ratios derived from the drainage area both to the lake area and to the lake volume. This indicates that the terrestrial supply of mercury to lakes has an important impact on enhanced mercury uptake in fish. Evans (1986) concluded from studies of lakes in south-central Ontario (Canada) that the most likely source of recent mercury found in lake sediments was outwash of anthropogenic metal deposited in the catchments.

The present annual atmospheric deposition on small catchment areas in southern Sweden is, on average, about 10 times higher than the output via run-off waters. Obviously, mercury is accumulating in forest soils in Sweden at the present atmospheric deposition rate (Iverfeldt and

Johansson, 1988). The content of mercury in the mor layer of forest soil shows high concentrations in the southern part of Sweden and in areas along the Bothnian coast (see figure 2) (Andersson, 1987).

Anthropogenic emissions of mercury into the atmosphere, mainly during this century, have affected the amount and concentrations of mercury in the mor layer. In Sweden, the elevated concentrations in parts of central regions are influenced by emissions, mostly from the chloralkali industry (figure 3), while the levels in the southern part of Sweden are probably mainly caused by long-range transport and emissions from other European countries. Calculated on a real basis, the mor layer contains about 2.5 kg/km^2. The amount in the northernmost parts is only about one fifth of that in the south (Andersson, 1987).

The increased content of mercury in forest soils may have an effect on the organisms and the biological processes in the soils. Laboratory studies of metal toxicity in soils (Stadelmann and Santshi-Fuhrimann, 1987) have shown, for example, that mercury is the metal most toxic to micro-organisms. The specific toxicity of metals declined in the following order:

$$Hg >> Cr \approx V > Tl > Mo >> Cu > Co > Cd > Ni >> Pb >> Zn$$

As for the microbiological processes in soil, a guideline value of a total content of mercury in soil of 0.4 to 0.5 parts per million was proposed. These concentrations are already found today in forest soils in parts of southern and central Sweden.

With the present state of knowledge, however, it is not yet possible to assess a critical concentration for mercury in soils. However, since mercury contamination is a large-scale pollution problem and the turnover of mercury in soils is extremely slow, it is important to prevent the content of mercury in soils from increasing any further.

V. CRITICAL LOAD

Owing to air pollution, the content of mercury in fish is significantly increased in a large part of Scandinavia and North America. A large number of lakes exceed the "blacklisting limits". This is an unacceptable situation. A reasonable goal would be that mercury levels in fish from the large majority of waters should not exceed 0.5 mg/kg, that is the blacklisting limit used in many countries. For most people, no restrictions would then be necessary for consumption of fish from waters with no direct outlet of pollutants. Diet recommendations would, however, probably still be necessary for pregnant women.

To obtain a general decrease in the mercury content in fish, the atmospheric deposition of mercury of anthropogenic origin has to be reduced.

A reduction of the atmospheric deposition of mercury will result in a comparatively rapid (years), but limited, effect on the mercury content in fish owing to a decreased load directly on the lake surface. In order to obtain the goal and to ensure that the content in fish will not increase in future decades, the transport of mercury from the catchment area must also be reduced. This means that the atmospheric deposition has to be reduced to levels less than the output from the catchment area. In figure 4, the principal effect of a reduction of mercury deposition on the mercury content in fish is illustrated. The critical load of mercury can be defined as the atmospheric load where the input to the forest soils is less than the output and, consequently, where the mercury content in the top soil layers and the transport of mercury to the surface waters starts to decrease. The critical load for mercury cannot be determined accurately today. The redistribution processes of mercury within catchment areas and the output via re-emission from the soils are major gaps in present knowledge. Probably a reduction somewhere in the range of 50 to 90 per cent from present atmospheric deposition has to be obtained.

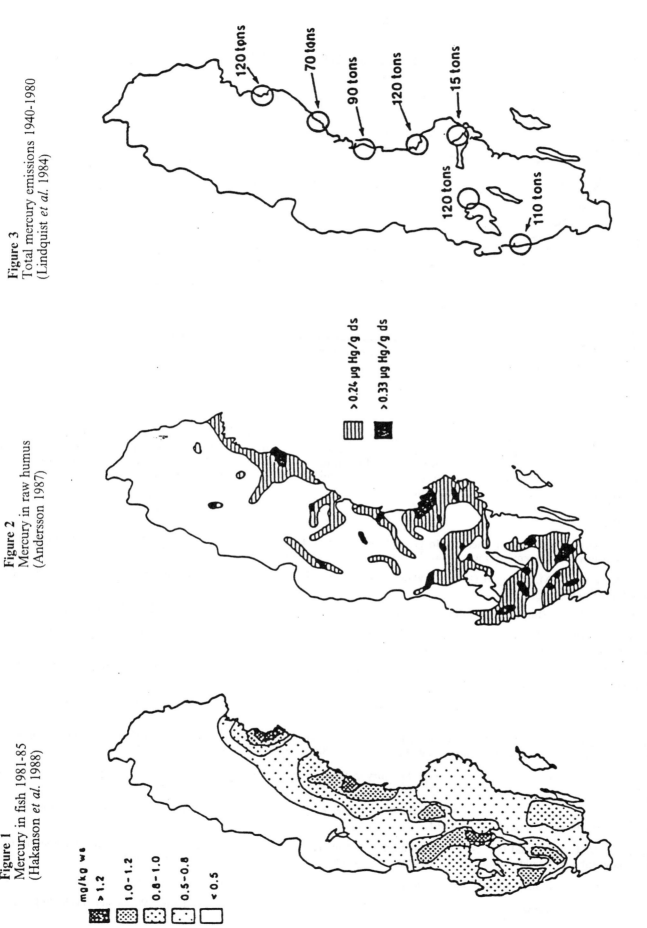

Figure 3
Total mercury emissions 1940-1980
(Lindquist *et al.* 1984)

120 tons
70 tons
90 tons
120 tons
15 tons
120 tons
110 tons

Figure 2
Mercury in raw humus
(Andersson 1987)

> 0.24 μg Hg/g ds

> 0.33 μg Hg/g ds

Figure 1
Mercury in fish 1981-85
(Hakanson *et al.* 1988)

mg/kg ws

> 1.2

1.0 – 1.2

0.8 – 1.0

0.5 – 0.8

< 0.5

Maps have been provided by the Government of Sweden and are reproduced as submitted.
The boundaries do not imply official endorsement or acceptance by the United Nations.

FIGURE 4

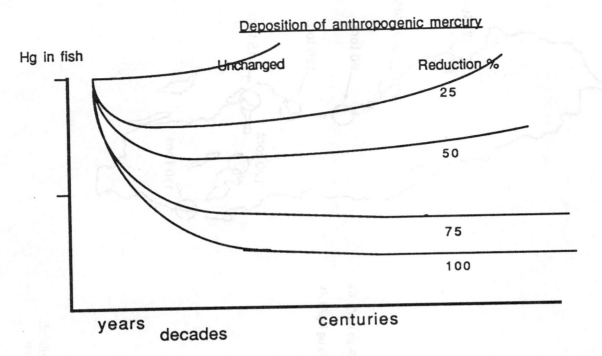

The principle of the relation between the atmospheric deposition of mercury and mercury content in fish. In this assessment, it is supposed that a reduction of 50-75 per cent of the anthropogenic mercury deposition is needed to achieve a balanced input/output budget for soils. The time schedule is mainly dependent on the amount of anthropogenic mercury stored in the soils and geological, chemical and hydrological properties of the catchment area controlling the transport of mercury in the soils.

REFERENCES

Aastrup, M. (1986). Occurrence of mercury in groundwater. In: O. Lindqvist, K. Johansson and B. Timm. Mercury, occurrence and turnover in the environment. Nat. Environ. Prot. Bd. (Sweden), progress report 3256.

Ahmed, R., K. May and M. Stoeppler (1987). Wet deposition of mercury and methyl mercury from the atmosphere. Sci. Total Environ. 60: p.249-261.

Akielaszek, J.J. and T.A. Haines (1981). Mercury in the muscle tissue of fish from three northern Maine lakes. 27: p.201-208.

Andersson, A. (1979). Mercury in soils. In: J.O. Nriagu, (Ed), The biogeochemistry of Mercury in the Environment. Elsevier/North Holland Biomedical Press: p.79-106.

Andersson, A. (1987). Inventory of the mercury content in the raw humus layer of forest soil. (In Swedish). Nat. Environ. Prot. Bd. (Sweden) Stencil. 26 pp.

Benes, P., E.T. Gjessing and E. Steinnes (1976). Interactions between humus and trace elements in fresh water. Water Res. 10: p.711-716

Björklund, I. and L. Norling (1979). Effects of air-borne mercury on concentrations in pike and sediments around a chlor-alkali plant. (In Swedish, English summary), Nat. Environ. Prot. Bd. (Sweden) PM 1090: 72 pp.

Björklund, I., H. Borg and K. Johansson (1984). Mercury in Swedish lakes - its regional distribution and causes. Ambio 13: p.118-121.

Björnberg, A., L. Häkanson and K. Lundbergh (1988). A theory on the mechanisms regulating the bioavailability of mercury in natural waters. Environ. Pollut. 49: p.53-61.

Bloom, N. and W.F. Fitzgerald (1988). Determination of volatile mercury species at the picogram level by low-termperature gas chromatography with cold-vapour atomic fluoroescence detection. Anal. Chim. Acta 208: p.151-161.

Brosset, C. (1982). Total airborne mercury and its possible origins. Water, Air and Soil Pollution 17: p.37-50.

Brosset, C. (1983). Transport of airborne mercury emitted by coal burning into aquatic systems. Water Sci. Tech. Bull. 15: p.59-66.

Brosset, C. (1987). The behavior of mercury in the physical environment. Water, Air and Soil Pollution 34: p.145-166.

Brosset C. and A. Iverfeldt (1989). Interaction of solid gold with mercury in ambient air. Water, Air and Soil Pollution 43: p.147-168

Brouzes R., R. McLean and G. Tomlinson (1977). The link between the pH of natural waters and the mercury content of fish. Domtar Research Centre Report, Senneville, Quebec.

Drabaeck, I. and A. Iverfeldt (1988). Elemental analysis: Mercury (Chapter 7). In: Evaluation of analytical methods in biological systems, M. Stoeppler (Ed). Techniques and Instrumentation in Analytical Chemistry, subseries vol. 4, Elsevier Science Publ. (Amsterdam).

Ek, J. (1986). Mercury in soil and stream peat/stream moss at geochemical reference stations. (In Swedish). Sveriges Geologiska Undersökning, BRAP 86007: 39 pp.

Evans, R.D. (1986). Sources of mercury contamination in the sediments of small headwater lakes in south-central Ontario, Canada. Arch. Environ. Contam. Toxicol 15: p.505-512.

Ferrara, R. et al. (1982). The biogeochemical cycle of mercury in the Mediterranean. Part 2: Mercury in the atmosphere, aerosol and in rainwater of a northern Tyrrhenian area. Environ. Technol. Lett 3: p.449-456.

Fitzgerald, W.F., G.A. Gill and A.D. Hewitt (1983). Air-sea exchange of mercury. In: Trace Metals in Sea Water, (C.S. Wong et al., eds.), Plenum Press, (New York): p.297-315.

Fitzgerald, W.F. (1986). Cycling of mercury between the atmosphere and oceans. P. Buat-Ménard (ed.). In: The Role of Air-Sea Exchange in Geochemical Cycling: p.363-408. By D. Reidel Publishing Company.

Förstner, U. and G.T.W. Wittmann, (1981). Metal pollution in the aquatic environment, Springer-Verlag (Berlin).

Glass, G.E. et al. (1986). Airbone mercury in precipitation in the Lake Superior region. J. Great Lakes Res. 12 (1): p.37-51, Internat. Assoc. Great Lakes Res. (1986).

Heit, M., Y. Tan and C. Klusek (1981). Anthropogenic trace elements and polycyclic aromatic hydrocarbon levels in sediment cores from two lakes in the Adirondack acid lake region. Water, Air and Soil Pollution 15: p.441-464.

Huckabee, J.W., C. Feldman and Y. Talmi (1974). Mercury concentrations in fish from the Great Smokey Mountains national park. Analytica Chimica Acta 70: p.41-47.

Huckabee, J.W., J.W. Elwood and S.G. Hildebrand (1979). Accumulation of mercury in freshwater biota. In: J.O. Nriagu, (Ed), The biogeochemistry of Mercury in the Environment. Elsevier/North Holland Biomedical Press: p.277-296.

Häkanson, L. (1974). Mercury in some Swedish lake sediments. Ambio 3: p.37-43.

Häkanson, L. (1975). Mercury in lake Vänern - present status and prognosis. (In Swedish, English summary). Nat. Environ. Prot. Bd. (Sweden) PM 563: 121 pp.

Häkanson, L. (1984). Metals in fish and sediment from the river Kolbäcksan water system, Sweden. Arch. Hydrobiol. 101: p. 373-400.

Häkanson, L., A. Nilsson and T. Andersson (1988). Mercury in fish in Swedish lakes. Environ. Pollut. 49: p.145-162.

Iverfeldt, A. and K. Johansson (1988). Mercury in run-off water from small watersheds. Verh. Internat. Verein. Limnol. 23: p.1626-1632.

Iverfeldt, A. and H. Rodhe (1988). Atmospheric transport and deposition of mercury in the Nordic countries. Progress report prepared for the Nordic Council of Ministers. Swedish Environmental Research Institute (Göteborg). No. L 87-285.

Jackson, T.A. et al. (1980). Experimental study of trace metal in soft water lakes at different pH levels. Can. J. Fish. Aquat. Sci. 37: p.387-402.

Jensen, A. (1988). Bestemmelse af kviksolv depositionsrater i Norden ud fra analyse og datering af hojmoser. Statusrapport (in Swedish). Nordic Council of Ministers, Copenhagen.

Johansson, K., O. Lindqvist and B. Timm (1988). Mercury, occurence and turnover of mercury in the environment. Nat. Environ. Prot. Bd. (Sweden) report 3470: 37 pp.

Johansson, K. (1985). Mercury in sediment in Swedish forest lakes. Verh. Internat. Verein. Limnol. 22: p.2359-2363.

Johnson, M.G., L.R. Culp and S.E. George (1986). Temporal and spatial trends in metal loadings to sediments of the Turkey lakes, Ontario. Can. J. Fish: Aquat. Sci. 43: p.754-762.

Kjellström, T. et al. (1986). Physical and mental development of children with prenatal exposure to mercury from fish. Nat. Environ. Prot. Bd. (Sweden) Report 3080: 96 pp.

Lindqvist, O. and H. Rodhe (1985). Atmospheric mercury - a review. Tellus 37 B: p.136-159.

Lindqvist, O. (1986). Fluxes of mercury in the Swedish Environment. Contributions from waste incineration. Waste manage. Res. 4: P.35-44.

Lindqvist, O. *et al.* (1984). Mercury in the Swedish environment, global and local sources. Nat. Environ. Prot. Bd (Sweden) report 1816: 105 pp.

Lodenius, M., A. Seppänen and A. Uusi-Rauva (1983). Sorption and mobilization of mercury in peat soil. Chemosphere 12: p.1575-1581.

Lodenius, M. (1987). Factors affecting the mobilization of mercury from coal. In: S.E. Lindberg and T.C. Hutchinson (eds.). Heavy metals in the environment. Proc. Internat. Conf., New Orleans, U.S.A.

Nat. Inst. for Public Health. (1970). Methyl mercury in fish, a toxicologic-epidemiologic evaluation of risks. Nordisk Hygienisk Tidskrift supplement 4: p.75-79.

Nordberg, G.F., R.A. Goyer and T.W. Clarkson (1985). Impact of effects of acid precipitation on toxicity of metals. Environ. Health Persp. 63: p.169-180.

Pheiffer Madson, P. (1981). Peat bog records of atmospheric mercury deposition. Nature 293: p.127-129.

Quellet, M. and H.G. Jones (1983). Historical changes in acid precipitation and heavy metals deposition originating from fossil fuel combustion in eastern-north America as revealed by lake sediment geochemistry. Wat. Sci. Tech. 15: p.115-130.

Rada, R.G., *et al.* (1989). Recent increases in atmospheric deposition of merucry to north-central Wisconsin lakes inferred from sediment analyses. Arch. Environ. Contam. Toxicol. 18: p.175-181.

Rae, J.E. and S.R. Aston (1982). The role of suspended soils in the estuarine geochemistry of mercury. Water Res. 16: p.649-654.

Rekolainen, S., M. Verta and A. Liehu (1986). The effect of airborne mercury and peatland drainage on sediment mercury contents in some Finnish forest lakes. Publications of the Water Research Institute, National Board of Waters, Finland, no. 65: p.11-21.

Schindler, D.W. *et al.* (1980). Effects of acidification on mobilization of heavy metals and radionuclides from the sediments of a freshwater lake. Can. J. Fish. Sci. 37: p.373-377.

Schnitzer, M. and H. Kerndorf (1981). Reactions of fulvic acid with metal ions. Water, Air and Soil Pollution 15: p: 97-108.

Sheffy, T.B. (1987). A review of mercury in Wisconsin's environment: recommendations for studying and identifying the cause of the problem. Wisconsin Dept. of Natural Resources (PUBL-AM-021).

Slemr, F., W. Seiler and G. Schuster (1981). Latitudinal distribution of mercury over the Atlantic Ocean. J. Geophys. Res. 86: p.1159-1166.

Stadelmann, F.X. and Santschi-Fuhrimann (1987). Beitrag zur abstuetzung von schwermetall-richtwerten im boden mit hilfe von bodenatmungsmessungen. Swiss federal research station for agricultural chemistry and hygiene of environment, Liebefeld, CH-3097.

Strohal, P. and D. Huljev (1971). Investigation of mercury pollutant interaction with humic acids by means of radiotracers. Proc. Symp. Nucl. Techniques in Environ. Pollution (Vienna): p. 439-446.

Suns, K., C. Curry and D. Russel (1980). The effects of water quality and morphometric parameters on mercury uptake by yearling yellow perch. Ministry of the Environment, Ontario, Technological Report LTS 80-1.

Tolonen, K. and T. Jaakola (1983). History of lake acidification and air pollution studied on sediments in South Finland. Ann. Bot. Fennici 20: p.57-78.

Verta, M., *et al.* (1986). The origin and level of mercury in Finnish forest lakes. Publications of the Water Research Institute, National Board of Waters, Finland, no. 65: p.21-31.

Wren, D.C. and H.R. MacCrimmon (1983). Mercury in the sunfish, Lepomis gibbosus, relative to pH and other environmental variables of precambrian shield lakes. Can. J. Fish. Sci. vol 40: p.1737-1744.

Xun, L., N.E.R. Campbell and J.W.M. Rudd (1987). Measurements of specific rates of net methyl mercury production in the water column and surface sediments of acidified and circumneutral lakes. Can. J. Fish. Aquatic. Sci. vol. 44: p.750-757.

Part FOUR

EFFECTS OF SOME HEAVY METALS RELATED TO LONG-RANGE ATMOSPHERIC TRANSPORT

This part deals with biological and chemical effects of metals in the environment caused by long-range transport and regional deposition. Special emphasis has been put on effects of metals in temperate forest ecosystems. Literature reviews have been prepared to serve as background documents for assessment of the potential long-term effects of atmospheric deposition of some heavy metals on forest soils, natural vegetation and water (Bergkvist *et al.*, Balsberg Pahlsson, Tyler, Baath, Bengtsson *et al.*, Allard *et al.*, Borg and Johansson, 1988).

The long-range atmospheric transport of air pollutants has been well documented. Southern Scandinavia belongs to those areas which are appreciably affected by air pollutants derived from distant source regions. A substantial amount of work has been carried out in Norway and Sweden in order to study the atmospheric supply of trace elements from other areas, the regional deposition patterns of these elements, and their significance with respect to contamination of terrestrial environments (e.g. Rühling *et al.*, 1987; Steinnes, 1987; Ross, 1987). This report aims at assessing the environmental consequences of atmospheric deposition of metals in rural areas affected mainly by long-range transport. However, while data exist on concentrations and fluxes in rural areas there is practically no information on biological effects at near-background levels. These have been assessed from results of laboratory research and field gradient studies in polluted areas.

A critical load is defined as "a quantitative estimate of the exposure to one or more pollutants below which significant harmful effects on specified sensitive elements of the environment do not occur according to present knowledge" (Protocol concerning the Control of Emissions of Nitrogen Oxides or their Transboundary Fluxes, 1988). Effects caused by the exposure of organisms to heavy metal deposition may be related to either current deposition rates or to accumulated amounts in the ecosystem; many effects are certainly being related to both (Tyler *et al.*, 1989). The concept of a "sustainable world" implies the protection of the environment in a long-term perspective (whether several decades or several hundreds of years). The critical load concept should therefore also include effects in the future, that is, the critical load should be the highest long-term deposition not causing significant adverse future effects.

I. ATMOSPHERIC TRANSPORT AND DEPOSITION

For a majority of trace elements, emissions from anthropogenic sources significantly exceed emissions from natural sources (Pacyna, 1986). Anthropogenic emissions of a number of elements have been estimated in a 150 square kilometre grid over Europe using specific emission factors and statistical information on industrial production and energy consumption. Calculations using a trajectory model show that measured concentrations of trace elements from long-range transport at Birkenes in southern Norway can be related to calculated anthropogenic emissions for a number of elements, e.g. V, Pb, Cd, Mn, Cr (Pacyna, 1984) and As, Sb, V, Zn (Pacyna, 1989). The concentrations of many trace elements in southern Scandinavia may be one order of magnitude higher in air masses that have passed over the European continent compared to concentrations in air masses from the North Atlantic region (Lannefors, 1983).

A method using a combination of pattern recognition technique and principal component analysis has been used to study the influence of aerosol long-range transport to Scandinavia on the basis of cascade impactor measurements. The results indicate that contributions from foreign sources to the trace element concentrations in Sweden vary from 50 to 90 per cent depending on the element (Martinsson, 1984).

Increased concentrations of trace elements have been found at remote regions far away from industrial sources. These concentrations are episodic, which leads to the conclusion that the occurrence of these pollutants at remote locations is due to long-range atmospheric transport from the source regions (Pacyna, 1987). Source-receptor relationships calculated for trace elements emitted from various sources in Europe and measured at a number of remote locations confirm this (Pacyna, 1989).

Aerosol studies have shown that anthropogenic emissions from sources in western Europe, Eurasia and North America may pollute the Arctic. The levels of air pollutants in the Norwegian Arctic are within the range of levels observed in other remote regions, but are one order of magnitude higher than in Antarctica. Even the non-episodic concentrations of elements at Spitsbergen (Norway) are at least one order of magnitude higher than in Antarctica.

The deposition of toxic elements by orographic precipitation is an important step in their accumulation in the environment. The highest concentrations of Pb in soil and mosses in Norway are found some 20 kilometres inland of the south-eastern shoreline, an area with relatively little car traffic. Situated a few hundred metres above sea level, this area receives about 2,000 mm precipitation per year, mostly with polluted air from the central parts of Europe. In these orographic precipitation areas, deposition maxima are found for several trace elements. The south-western and western coast of Norway receives more precipitation, but the Atlantic air is relatively clean, and the deposition of pollutants is lower. Similar deposition maxima can be found in any orographic precipitation area which is frequently exposed to polluted air masses, for example in the central parts of Europe.

Routine monitoring of trace metals in atmospheric precipitation was begun in 1983 at nine sites in Sweden. The wet deposition of trace metals is highest in southern Sweden and decreases northward by a factor of 3 to 5. Trace metal concentrations in precipitation reported from other rural areas, for example in Ontario (Canada) the Appalachian Mountains (United States) and at a mid-Atlantic site are similar to those found in Sweden. In Ontario, a north-south gradient similar to that for Sweden, was found for Pb. Only data sets where special care has been taken to avoid sample contamination have been included in this comparison. Cd, Cu and Pb concentrations at rural sites in the Federal Republic of Germany are about twice the values in southern Sweden. In contrast, Fe and Zn concentrations are approximately the same

(Ross, 1987). Trace metal concentrations in precipitation reported elsewhere are of the same order of magnitude (Bergkvist et al., 1988).

Several studies have shown that surveys of metal concentration in mosses may be a valuable means of mapping metal deposition (Tyler, 1989; Rühling, 1984; Rühling et al., 1987). To assess any temporal or spatial changes in atmospheric trace metal deposition, a survey of metal concentrations in mosses has been performed every five years in Sweden since 1969/1970. A first joint moss survey of the Nordic countries and adjacent areas in the northern part of the Federal Republic of Germany was made in 1985 (Rühling et al., 1987). Two moss species were used: *Hylocomium splendens* and *Pleurozium schreberi.*

The regional background deposition pattern shows for all metals a decreasing gradient from relatively high values in the southern parts of Scandinavia to low values towards the north. The gradient is steep for As, Cd, Pb and V, whereas the concentrations of Cr, Cu, Fe, Ni, and to some extent Zn, show weaker gradients. The metals Cd, Pb, and Zn, which originate from anthropogenic emission sources, are found in lower concentrations in the arctic regions of Greenland, Iceland and Svalbard. Conversely, As, Cr, Cu, Fe and V, originating also from soil dust or volcanic activity, are found in high concentrations in sparsely vegetated regions. Except for Cd, no significant differences were found between the concentration levels in Denmark and the northern part of the Federal Republic of Germany. Important local enhancements of the concentrations in moss were found superimposed on the regional background pattern in areas influenced by local sources.

Studies of heavy metals in moss reveal a general increase in concentrations in many regions up to 1970. Later, this increase was superceded by a decrease in concentration levels of most metals. In central and southern Sweden and in southern Norway the concentrations of Cd and Pb in moss have been reduced by about 50 per cent during the past decade. The decrease in concentrations for most metals in large areas is mainly due to emission control or the closure of old polluting industrial plants. This reduction affects local as well as long-range transport. In the case of Pb the decrease is due to a reduction of lead content in petrol.

Peat cores from 21 ombrotrophic bogs distributed all over Norway have been investigated with respect to vertical distribution of Cr, Co, Ni, Cu, Zn, As, Se, Cd, Sb, Hg and Pb. Results for surface peat samples indicate that atmospheric deposition rates for As, Cd, Sb and Pb in the southern areas of the country are about 10 times those in the far north. Similar but less pronounced north-south gradients are apparent for the other elements. Surface concentrations of the above four elements in southern bogs are more than 20 times those at 50 cm depth, and their depth distribution profiles are very similar, indicating strong atmospheric supply from a common source region during industrial times. Data for Se suggest atmospheric supply both from natural and anthropogenic sources (Hvatum, 1987).

Considering the evidence from precipitation and aerosol measurements in different parts of the world and results from atmospheric transport modelling, it is evident that long-range transport of metals from source areas contributes significantly to the deposition load over large areas of the northern hemisphere. This conclusion is further supported by results of retrospective studies in rural areas, showing a relation between industrial activities and metal concentrations in, for example, mosses and in peat profiles.

II. EFFECTS ON FOREST ECOSYSTEMS

A. Bryophytes and lichens

Of the main biological groups in a forest ecosystem, bryophytes and lichens are subjected to maximum exposure to direct metal deposition. The bryophyte and lichen flora are influenced by low levels of heavy metal pollution. Effects on the total species composition in bryophytes have been measured at two to three times the current baseline deposition of Cu + Zn. Slightly higher degrees of pollution were needed to influence the epiphytic lichen flora (Tyler *et al*, 1989).

Field studies have shown that several species of bryophytes might be affected by increased concentrations of copper in their tissues. A critical level for Cu in, for instance *Hylocomium splendens* and *Pleurozium schreberi*, seems to be 70 to 80 mg/kg dry weight. This is about 10 times the background concentration of Cu in southern Scandinavia. There is evidence that the most sensitive lichens are affected at a concentration of around 90 mg/kg dry weight. However, large differences between species are evident in both mosses and lichens, several forms being characterized by extreme tolerance to heavy metals (Tyler *et al.*, 1989).

From experimental studies using metal salt solutions, it may be concluded that the relative toxicity in bryophytes, at equal concentrations, of the heavy metals most often studied decreases in the order:

$$Hg > Cu, Cd > Pb > Zn \quad (Tyler, 1988).$$

A comparison of critical levels with deposition data and concentration levels in rural areas only influenced by long-range transport indicates that adverse effects of heavy metals on lichens and bryophytes are not very probable at the present regional deposition rate in Scandinavia. However, it should be noted that effects on the most sensitive species have been recorded at pollution levels which are not unusual in rural areas in, for instance, the Federal Republic of Germany.

B. Vascular plants

Vascular plants may be exposed to metals from the atmosphere via direct interception by the above-ground biomass or via the root system. In Norway, the geographical distribution of the heavy-metal content in vascular plants in coniferous forest ecosystems was related to the atmospheric deposition of these metals. Cu showed no significant regional difference. The Zn levels were generally higher, and Pb and Cd levels in southern Norway were about five times those in central Norway (Steinnes 1987). Also in other studies the metal content in different tree compartments has been found to correlate with the pollution load (e.g. Wagner and Müller, 1972; Heinrichs and Mayer, 1980; Steinnes, 1987).

Vascular plants with only limited uptake through the above-ground biomass are partly protected against direct or immediate influence of the metals by chemical immobilization mechanisms of the soil. The same mechanisms, however, are responsible for the long-term accumulation of heavy metals in the rhizosphere, which gradually may bring about an increase in the heavy-metal exposure of the plant roots (Tyler *et al.*,1989).

Root uptake differs greatly between metals. To a certain extent roots are capable of discriminating against toxic metals such as Pb and Cd whereas the uptake of nutrients such as Cu is often favoured. Thus, measurements of metal fluxes in spruce forests in rural areas in southern Sweden (Bergkvist, 1986) showed that cycling between soil and vegetation was of great importance to the ecosystem budgets of mainly K, Ca and Mn. This internal recycling was also of major importance for Cu, Cr, Mg, Ni and Zn. These metal ions are readily taken up by tree roots and recycled to the soil, either leached from the needles or returned as litter.

A contrasting element was Pb. Its internal recycling is very limited. The needles absorb Pb from the atmosphere very effectively. Atmospheric deposition of Pb to the canopy is the dominant source of Pb uptake in plants. Moreover, the root uptake of Cd is lower than the contribution from the atmosphere to the ecosystem. In polluted areas the situation is different as will be explained below.

Precipitation passing through the canopy is often enriched with heavy metals. The extent of this enrichment in the throughfall varies greatly between metals, tree species, stand structure and soil fertility and with the pollution load. Interception is usually greater in conifers than in deciduous trees on account of a larger aerosol-trapping leaf area (Bergkvist, 1988). An increased throughfall deposition of metals has been noted in areas with a high supply of metals in the top soil, either owing to a big store (accumulated during earlier pollution periods) or owing to a higher metal solubility by the influence of acidification or other soil factors (Bergkvist, 1988; Lamersdorf, 1988). This indicates that the metal availability in the top soil is determining the root uptake and the internal cycling of metals.

It has been suggested that the deposition of heavy metals may be contributing to forest damage in central Europe (Lamersdorf, 1988; Ulrich, 1984). Trace metals in forest ecosystems may be enriched in fine roots, in the humus layer and also in the cortex (Lamersdorf, 1988). However, the accumulation of metals in the cortex - a part of the plant that is physiologically inactive - is probably not an important factor.

There is no firm field evidence that regional deposition levels of heavy-metals causes forest damage. Adverse effects of heavy-metal ions (Cd, Cu, Pb, Zn) on vascular plants in nutrient solutions have been observed from concentrations two to ten times those of acid forest soil solutions at sites without local pollution (Bahlsberg Pahlsson, 1988). The field relevance of experiments using nutrient solutions is difficult to assess. Therefore, leaf tissue concentrations have been suggested as an alternative measurement tool. Critical leaf tissue concentrations have been estimated at two to ten times those found in leaves from growing trees in rural areas (Balsberg Pahlsson, 1988).

Possible effects of mycorrhiza on plant growth in heavy metal-polluted soil is a question of increasing concern (Tyler et al., 1989). Heavy metals may exhibit effects on mycorrhizal fungi and on the interaction between fungi and plants. Mycorrhizal fungi may be sensitive to increased levels of heavy metals. High levels of metals sometimes, but not always, decrease the level of mycorrhizal infection in a plant, which in turn may or may not enhance metal uptake in the roots. Often, an increased metal tolerance of the plant is found with mycorrhiza present, usually in connection with a lower uptake of metal to the plant compared to non-mycorrhizal plants. Ectomycorrhiza has been found to increase growth and facilitate establishment of seedlings in metal-polluted soil (Tyler et al., 1989). Accumulation of metals in ectomycorrhizal roots indicates that the fungal symbiont may bind metals in forms not available to the plant. However, mycorrhiza may enhance plant uptake of Zn and Cu, when these metals are present at low concentrations.

The effects of heavy metals differ widely between different types of mycorrhiza. Mycorrhizal infection may be inhibited at concentrations in the soil of, for example, 45 mg Zn/kg, or 19 to 34 mg Cu/kg of soil. Bell et al. (1988) took field samples and found decreased incidence of ectomycorrhizal root tips in soils naturally enriched with Cu, Pb and Zn. The organic and A horizons of soil in metal-enriched sites had metal contents two to six times those in control sites (Baath, 1988).

C. Effects on soil organisms and processes

General indications of heavy-metal effects on soil organisms have already been obtained from studies of soil biological processes, including the rates of litter decomposition, soil respiration, nitrogen mineralization and the activity of enzymes in soils variously polluted by heavy metals.

Effects on the biology of coniferous forest litter and mor soils have been studied in gradients at a smelter (Cu + Pb + Zn + As) and at a brass foundry (Cu + Zn) in Sweden (Tyler et al., 1989). Significant activity depressions (20-40 per cent), compared to controls, were measured when the heavy metal concentrations amounted to a few (2-10) times those of regional baseline (control) samples. The results also indicated that the toxic effects were augmented at low levels of soil pH.

Studies of soil biological processes in heavy-metal-polluted areas have shown that adverse effects on microbial activity may occur already from a heavy-metal concentration of the topsoil corresponding to about three times the current baseline concentration of comparable soil samples in southern Scandinavia.

Although effects on micro-organisms are more difficult to assess than the total biological activity of soils, activity depressions certainly reflect changes in the functioning of the decomposer communities. However, negative effects on micro-organisms, both on functional groups and on the species level, have mainly been recorded at higher heavy-metal concentrations in the soil than those found to affect respiration rate or enzymatic activity.

Altered community structure of micro-organisms has been detected from levels about four times the baseline Cu + Zn concentration while a reduction in sporophore formation of macro-fungi is noted from about three times the baseline heavy-metal concentration of forest topsoils (Tyler et al., 1989).

A common effect of metal contamination in all groups of soil animals is a decrease in species diversity (Bengtsson et al., 1988). The lowest ("critical") concentrations reported to cause significant effects in the most sensitive groups of soil animals have been observed from a few times the estimated baseline concentrations in litter.

Usually, however, diversity changes of the soil fauna are detectable only at relatively higher levels of pollution than those reported above. Many species of soil animals have been recorded from heavily polluted areas and seem to be quite resistant to elevated concentrations of metals (Bengtsson et al., 1988). With the present state of knowledge it is difficult to predict which types of soils will be sensitive. Lowering the pH can have two different effects: one is the increased leaching of certain metals, making soil concentrations lower. However, lowering pH can also increase bio-availability and toxicity.

D. Birds and mammals

The heavy-metal content in organs or tissues of organisms may give some indication of their degree of exposure to heavy metals. This has been shown in many studies. For example, gradient studies in an immission area around a copper smelter showed that the concentrations of As, Cd, Hg, Pb, Se in birds correlate with the distance from the source (Nyholm, 1987). Elevated concentrations of six to sixty times baseline values were recorded. Another example is that organs of hares from a polluted area contained two to three times as much lead as those from uncontaminated areas and organs of roe deer three to four times as much. Even though the cadmium content in kidneys was mainly related to the age of the animals, it was much higher in game from the contaminated area. In the same study (from the Federal Republic of Germany) arsenic con-

centrations in game organs were up to eight times those in a polluted area in background data (Holm, 1979). High contents of Cd and Zn have been recorded in deer shot close to a zinc smelter in Pennsylvania (Sileo et al., 1984). Concentrations of Cu were not correlated, however, with the distance from the smelter.

The contents of As, Cd, Cu, Pb and Zn in organs or tissues of mammals and birds have been analysed in a variety of species in so-called background areas. Concentrations differ greatly between species living in the same environment. Cadmium may reach high levels in many species, especially in the kidney and in liver tissues. Animals and human subjects may accumulate cadmium during the whole life cycle (Cd biological half-life is several decades or more). Among mammals living in the wild, high levels of Cd have been found in the kidney of moose, deer and hare (Frank et al., 1981; Frank, 1982; Mattsson et al., 1981; Holt et al., 1978; Glooschenko et al., 1987).

Few studies have emphasized regional differences of metal content in birds and mammals which could shed light on the influence of the long-range transport of heavy metals. A regional study of trace element contents in liver tissues from Norwegian moose, reindeer and red deer demonstrated a north-south gradient for arsenic and to some extent also selenium and cadmium in moose and reindeer. This pattern was closely related to the regional distribution of these elements in forest moss (Froslie et al., 1984). As regards lead levels, a similar north-south gradient was found only in moose liver. The atmospheric deposition of lead, cadmium and some other relatively volatile elements in the southern-most part of Norway was around ten times that in the more northerly regions. About the same regional distribution of these elements has been found in surface soils and coniferous forest ecosystems and in liver tissues of lambs grazing natural pastures (Steinnes, 1987).

The highest levels of mercury, arsenic and lead were found in reindeer living on mountain plateaux, which may be explained by a high proportion of lichens in their food. It has been shown that lichens accumulate certain metals from the atmosphere (Tyler, 1988). With regard to cadmium, the correlation between levels in liver and moss was weak and scarcely significant. Cadmium is, however, an element that accumulates in the body with age. A possible north-south gradient may therefore have been confounded by age differences. Small or no significant regional differences were found for zinc or antimony.

It may be concluded from this investigation that the atmospheric deposition of mercury, lead, arsenic, cadmium and selenium contributed to the body burden of these elements in cervines from remote areas in Norway, and that the feeding habits of the animals influence the extent of this contribution (Froslie *et al.*, 1984).

A relation was shown between the level of pollution and the contents of Cd and Pb in the liver and kidneys of roe deer and hares in a study of five selected areas in Nordrhein-Westfalen (Federal Republic of Germany) (Lutz, 1985). In this case, the lowest levels of heavy metal contamination in the organs of both species were measured in "acid rain" forests.

In Ontario (Canada), levels of cadmium in the kidney, liver and muscle of moose were examined at five sampling sites (Glooschenko *et al.*, 1987). The study indicates that there are regional differences in the Cd contamination of wildlife in Ontario. A variety of factors, among them the buffering capacity of the soil, may influence the Cd uptake by herbivores (Glooschenko *et al.*, 1987). Also, results from a Quebec (Canada) study (Crête, 1987) points to the influence of a widespread presence of Cd in the environment that may be linked to acid precipitation.

The significance of a higher Cd contamination caused by a higher mobilization of Cd owing to acid precipitation is further strengthened by the results of a Swedish study. A clear concentration gradient was found for Cd accumulated in moose kidney from the north to the south-southwest (based on annual accumulation rates). This concentration pattern coincides with the degree of acidification of Swedish forest soils as well as with the distribution of wet deposited Cd (Frank, 1989). The conclusion from these studies is that the Cd wet deposition as well as the acidification may be important factors governing the Cd uptake in moose. However, other factors such as plant species composition and forage availability may also affect the food-chain transfer of Cd.

High concentrations of Cd in herbivores have been shown to correlate with the exposure to Cd from the diet (Tataruch, 1982; Lutz, 1985; Müller, 1985). For hare, the extent of agriculture (with the use of Cd-containing fertilizers) was found to be the main factor influencing the Cd content, along with age.

The influence of the diet might to some extent explain the high Cd concentrations in moose. Moose mostly browse leaves and twigs of trees and shrubs (Froslie et al., 1984). Twigs and bark have been shown to accumulate Cd, the concentrations being higher in polluted areas (e.g.

Lamersdorf, 1988). Furthermore, moose generally have a long life and Cd tends to accumulate with age (Müller, 1985).

The effects of low-level exposures to heavy metals on wildlife have not been assessed and no conclusions may be drawn about the significance of the long-range transport of metals. Few studies have been concerned with critical levels. The concentrations of Cd found in moose kidneys in south Sweden are about one fourth of those found to cause tissue damages in horse kidney (ca.75 mg/ kg fresh weight: Elinder, 1981). However, values in old moose in south Sweden exceed the recommendations given in a report submitted to the United States Fish and Wildlife Service (Eisler, 1985). This report states that: "the issue of the significance of cadmium residues in various body parts requires resolution. At this time, it appears that cadmium residues in the vertebrate kidney or liver that exceed 10 mg/kg fresh weight or 2 mg/kg in whole body fresh weight should be viewed as evidence of probable cadmium contamination. Elevated levels of 13-15 ppm tissue fresh weight probably represent a significant hazard to animals of the higher trophic levels, and residues of 200 ppm fresh weight kidney or more than 5 ppm whole animal fresh weight should be considered life-threatening".

The critical organ for chronic Cd toxicity is generally considered to be the kidney, although, in males, the testes may be severely affected by sublethal Cd exposure. When the Cd concentration reaches a critical value (100 to 200 ppm wet tissue in humans and experimental mammals), Cd-induced nephropathy occurs (Goyer, 1984; Nordberg, 1971: cited in Scheuhammer, 1987). In horse kidney, damage appears at about 350 mg/kg. For man, around 200 mg/kg (w.w.) in the kidneys is considered a critical level (Friberg *et al.*, 1986). Since the levels measured for moose in Scandinavia and in Canada are well below these values, a short-term negative impact is improbable, but the Cd abundancy in the environment indicates a potential problem (Crête, 1987).

No field data are available on the toxic effects of Cd on wild birds and mammals (Ros *et al.*, 1988). Even though Cd is accumulated in organs of vital importance, the effects being of a chronic rather than acute nature are not easily detected in animals living in the wild. The regional survey of moose in Sweden also included the analysis of 13 other elements, among them Pb, Cu, Zn, Co. No gradients were found for metals other than Cd (Frank, 1989).

There are few studies reporting concentrations in animals from remote sites representing true background values. It has been shown that bone concentrations of Pb in vertebrate tissues from the remote High Sierra were generally only 10 per cent of those in the controls of roadside studies, indicating that the roadside controls, often reported as background data, were themselves contaminated to a large degree. Furthermore, biogeochemical calculations suggest that even animals in remote areas have bone lead concentrations 50 to 500 times the natural background levels (EPA Air Quality Criteria for Lead, 1986).

Pb accumulates primarily in bones of mammals and birds. Of the soft tissues, kidneys accumulate the highest level (Scheuhammer, 1987). Kidney Pb-levels are regarded a good indicator of recent Pb exposure. The skeleton accumulates approximately 95 per cent of the total body burden of Pb in mammals. The Pb content in bone tissue is the best index of life-long exposure to Pb. Pb levels > 5 ppm dry weight in bones of adult wild birds would be indicative of some degree of increased environmental exposure to Pb (Finley and Dieter, 1978: cited in Scheuhammer, 1987).

Young birds are more susceptible to Pb than adults. Kidney Pb-levels of > 6 ppm wet weight has, for instance, been associated with growth impairments of kestrel nestlings, whereas > 15 µg/g were associated with impaired surival (Custer, 1984; Hoffman, 1985: cited in Scheuhammer, 1987).

The accumulation and toxicity of dietary Pb can be dramatically modified by the manipulation of dietary Ca levels in both mammals and birds. The increased uptake and retention of Pb observed under condition of deficient or marginal Ca intake results in the production of toxic effects at much lower levels of dietary Pb than would normally occur (Scheuhammer, 1987). In background areas, kidney Pb-levels normally do not exceed 1 to 5 ppm wet weight in birds and mammals, although skeleton levels indicate an increased environmental exposure to Pb.

Proposed criteria for the protection of various environmental compartments against chromium are disparate and often contradictory. Some of this confusion may be attributable to the inability to quantify chemical species and ionic states of Cr. While it is recognized that Cr is essential for some but not all species of mammals comparable, data for other groups of organisms are lacking. The significance of Cr residues in birds and mammals is unclear but according to Eisler (1986) concentrations of > 4 mg total Cr/kg dry weight should be viewed as presumptive evidence of Cr contamination, but no standpoint has been taken on potentially harmful concentrations. Very few background concentrations in birds or

mammals have been reported (e.g. Woolf, 1982; Connors, 1975; Jenkins, 1980). The concentrations are usually below 1 mg/kg dry weight. Exceptions are hair samples from mammals, which may accumulate very high concentrations of Cr.

The contents of pollutants in organs and tissues of indicator species are now being monitored in different countries as a tool to measure the environmental contamination and to assess the risk of ecological effects. Such monitoring data are very useful but they must be used with caution. Concentrations may differ greatly between organs and it is not certain that the analysed organ displays above-normal values even in severely poisoned organisms. In animals, elements that are not concentrated in the body (adsorption and excretion at equilibrium) are usually considered innocuous, though this should not be taken for granted in all cases. Also, some elements might accumulate biologically even at environmental concentrations that may be considered natural. This may sometimes be the case for Cd.

Moreover, caution is recommended when using concentration data for wild animals from background areas and polluted areas. These data usually represent healthy individuals in the population and are not necessarily representative of the entire population. Likewise, a biased selection may result from using game found dead by chance.

It is concluded that elevated concentrations of Cd and Pb in birds and mammals in background areas may be attributed to long-range transport. However, the concentrations do not normally exceed the lowest known effect levels. Metals other than Pb, Cd, and to some extent Cr, have not been included in this evaluation.

III. EFFECTS ON GROUND AND SURFACE WATER

Atmospheric deposition of metals may influence the quality of ground water and surface waters.

A. Ground water

The "natural" concentrations of heavy metals in unpolluted ground waters are partly related to the metal concentrations in the soil and the bedrock, but are also related to parameters such as pH, redox potential and natural organic complexing agents (Allard et al., 1988). Thus, natural background concentrations of metals in ground water cover a range of more than one order of magnitude.

Metal concentrations monitored in ground waters from various geological environments in "unpolluted" areas appear to be highly related to the presence and abundance of mineral phases rich in the corresponding element. Data give clear indications of a pronounced pH-dependence of metal concentrations. It is not possible to distinguish any "natural" background level or range representative of unpolluted waters solely from these data (Allard et al., 1988).

In areas polluted by refuse deposits, agriculture or mining, for example, the impact of the pollution on ground-water quality may be very pronounced. Ground water may also be influenced by atmospheric deposition in the vicinity of point sources. However, the heavy metal contribution from regional atmospheric deposition may not be distinguished from the background levels originating from natural sources or from the influence of acidification (Allard et al., 1988).

The mobility of a trace metal can, in most soil and ground-water systems, be regarded as a distribution process between an aquous phase (species in solution, organic or inorganic), a mobile solid phase (suspended colloidal) and a stationary solid phase. Minor changes in hydrochemical conditions, notably pH, can easily cause large shifts in this distribution (Allard et al., 1988).

Elevated concentrations of heavy metals in ground water may affect drinking-water quality, microbial processes in the ground water and aquatic ecosystems in streams and lakes. The concentration ranges of Cd, Cu, Pb and Zn in ground water from "unpolluted" areas in Scandinavia are well below drinking-water limit criteria (Allard et al., 1988). Concentrations higher than limit values for drinking water have been reported from other areas regarded as representative of unpolluted ground waters (Hermann and Neumann-Mahlkau, 1985: cited in Allard et al., 1988).

No critical load values have been assessed based on effects in ground water. The solubility and mobility of heavy metals in ground water is mainly determined by factors other than the regional atmospheric load of heavy metals, primarily by minerology and the soil acidification. It must be emphasized, though, that ground-water quality criteria should be set so as to comply with the environmental goal for surface waters.

B. Surface water

In a discharge area, ground water will mix with precipitation and form a mixed water, which constitutes the main water supply to forest lakes. When the discharge area is unsaturated, the precipitation infiltrates and percolates and mixes with the ground water. Thus metals are transported from the soil to streams and lakes. Metals are also transported to lakes via direct deposition from the air onto the lake surface. Both run-off and direct atmospheric deposition are significant.

Data on atmospheric deposition, transport via run-off water and contents in soil have been used to estimate the fluxes of Cu, Pb, Cd and Zn to Swedish forest lakes (Borg & Johansson, 1988). The dominating pathway for the input of Zn and Cd to lakes was via run-off from the drainage area (60 to 95 per cent, the higher amount representing acidified areas). The pH level in the soil was by far the most important factor regulating the mobility of these elements. For Pb, the direct deposition on the lake surface was more important (50 to 70 per cent). The transport of Pb from the soil is primarily associated with humic substances. The transport mechanisms for Cu are similar to those of Pb, but owing to the lower anthropogenic load, direct deposition is of less importance.

Most studies on heavy metals in surface waters have been concerned with the impact of local emissions. Background concentration levels in sea water and lake water have been assessed by different authors (Allard et al., 1988). The influence of airborne pollutants on water quality has been studied in Sweden (Borg, 1983). A geographical distribution pattern was observed for Zn, and to some extent also for Pb and Cd, with the concentrations highest in the south. However, pH and water colour were of major importance for the distribution of trace metals. Negative correlation with pH existed for total concentrations of Cd, Pb, Al, Mn and Zn. The dissolved (dialysable) metal fractions also increased with rising acidity. The concentration of humic substances influenced the distribution of Fe, Mn, Al, Pb, Cr, Co and As, as shown by positive correlations with water colour. The range of natural trace metal concentrations in unpolluted waters in southern and northern Sweden did not differ significantly between the the two study areas. The results cannot be used to assess the impact of regional atmospheric deposition of heavy metal on lake-water quality.

Analysis of sediments is a useful method to study the environmental pollution of heavy metals and has been used in numerous investigations (cf. review by Förstner and Wittman, 1981) including a large number of studies of the historical development of pollution (reviewed by Alderton, 1985). In recent years an increasing number of studies have been performed to evaluate the input of heavy metals to lakes with no local sources of contamination, in order to study the historical changes.

Increased content of metals in the top layers of sediment compared to the uncontaminated deeper layers is common regarding Cd, Hg, Pb and Zn and has been recorded even in remote areas. In Sweden, the regional impact of metals on lakes has been studied by sediment measurements (Johansson, 1988). An evident pollution pattern was found concerning Cd, Cu, Pb and Zn, indicating that there is a large-scale impact of these metals on Swedish forest lakes, caused by anthropogenic factors. Pb demonstrated the most widespread and pronounced pollution with marked enhancements in most parts of the country. The contamination of the top sediments gradually decreased towards the north. Non-polluted conditions were recorded for Cu and Zn in the northern region.

Concentrations of Cd, Cu, Pb and Zn in "unpolluted" lake and sea water in Scandinavia are generally lower than "lowest known effect levels" for aquatic organisms and those for example in Canadian guidelines for the protection of aquatic life. Concentrations exceeding these values have been reported from other "unpolluted" areas (Allard et al., 1988). However, in acidified lakes, extreme concentrations of Cd and Zn have been found which are about the same as those estimated as "lowest known effect levels" in aquatic ecosystems. Effects of high Cd and Zn concentrations cannot therefore be excluded in acidified lakes. No apparent effects of heavy metals have been observed in acidified lakes although no field studies have been performed to investigate this matter. Extreme values of Cu in lake water are also close to the "lowest known effect level" (Allard et al., 1988; Lithner, 1989).

The regional concentrations of heavy metals in sediments in southern Sweden influenced by long-range transport are elevated compared to estimated background levels with factors ranging from 1 to 5 for Cu, 4 to 40 for Pb, 5 to 30 for Cd and 3 to 10 for Zn (Johansson, 1988). No biological effects of heavy metals in sediments have been observed at these levels. It must be emphasized, though, that studies done of these low concentrations are scarce. Also, toxicity tests are usually performed in laboratories and with a single element. It cannot be excluded that more sensitive testing methods may reveal ecological

effects. Also, synergistic effects should be considered when assessing risks for the ecosystem.

Balance calculations show that the Pb and Cu contents in the top 0 to 50 cm soil layer are increasing at the present atmospheric deposition rate in rural areas. Assuming a relation between the metal store in the soil and the leaching rate, an increase in the Pb and Cu load on lakes may be predicted, all other factors remaining unchanged (Borg & Johansson, 1988). In several watershed studies, Zn and Cd display a positive budget leading to an accumulation in the soil. Acidic forests, though, release significant quantities of Zn and Cd. The mobility of Zn and Cd has been shown to increase with soil acidity. In addition, the soil type and the vegetation type seem to be of great importance for the leaching rates of metal (Bergkvist et al., 1988).

Soil acidity is the main factor controlling Zn and Cd leaching rates in Scandinavia, the influence of the atmospheric deposition load of these metals being of minor importance. At higher pH, the present atmospheric deposition level may lead to an increasing Zn and Cd content in the soil, which in the long-term may influence the leaching of these metals into surface waters.

IV. AGRICULTURAL PRODUCTS

Airborne metals may subject humans to direct exposure through inhalation or indirect exposure through ingestion of contaminated food. For the general population, the diet is the most important route of exposure to Pb and Cd. Absorption of Pb from the diet accounts for more than 80 per cent of the total exposure. Ninty-nine per cent of Cd absorption is from the diet (non-smokers) (Vahter, 1988).

Cadmium is the toxic element most likely to cause health problems if it is applied to agricultural land. Cd is not very toxic to higher plants, which means that it can accumulate, for example in lettuce leaves or tobacco, to very high levels without causing damage to the plant. Cd is not controlled by the soil-plant barrier, which limits plant uptake of many substances to levels substantially below concentrations which would be toxic to humans (Dean et al., 1985). Various studies of dietary intake of Cd show average daily intakes between 13 and 21 μg per day except for Japanwhere average values as high as 56 μg per day have been reported. Individual values may be much higher (Dean et al., 1985). The major part of the dietary intake of Cd comes from vegetables, including potatoes and cereals.

The limit accepted for daily intake is the FAO/WHO recommendation (WHO, 1972), equivalent to 60 to 70 µg per person per day (provisional tolerable weekly intake of 0.4 to 0.5 mg per person). In the Federal Republic of Germany the average dietary intake of Cd has been calculated at about 70 to 80 per cent of the recommended maximum (UBA, 1981). It was stated that the Cd load on humans had increased in the country during the past decades.

Anthropogenic sources of trace metals in cultivated soils include industries contributing to atmospheric deposition as well as fertilizers (mainly P-fertilizers), sewage, sludge, composted refuse and the like. Fertilizers and atmospheric deposition are the main Cd sources. In Sweden, atmospheric deposition amounted to about 40 per cent of total inflow of Cd to farmland in 1985 (Swedish Environmental Protection Board, 1987). In Denmark, the atmospheric inflow of Cd was estimated at approximately three times the fertilizer inflow of Cd over the 50- to 60-year period of examination (Tjell *et al.*, 1985). A flow-balance calculation for farmland in the Federal Republic of Germany indicated that the atmospheric deposition of Cd was a main contributor to the total Cd load on agricultural soils, amounting to about 30 per cent of the load as compared to 50 per cent from P-fertilizers (UBA, 1981).

Cadmium concentrations in the ploughing layer of normal agricultural soils are on an average 0.2 mg Cd kg^{-1} (dry weight) (range 0.03-2.3: Andersson, 1977) in the Scandinavian countries, while higher concentrations are normally found in more heavily industrialized countries. In the Netherlands and the Federal Republic of Germany, average concentrations in the topsoil of cultivated land registered 0.4-0.5 mg/kg^{-1} (Ros *et al.*, 1988; Tjell, 1983). The ploughing layer contains Cd concentrations two to three times those in the subsoil.

Inflow of Cd to agricultural areas greatly outweighs outflow, thus slowly creating increasing concentrations in the topsoil of agricultural areas in the industrialized countries (Tjell, 1983). Soil concentrations of Cd have been increasing during this century. Mass-balance studies in long-term fertilizer experimental fields in Denmark indicate an increase averaging 1 µg /kg soil per year, corresponding to 0.5 to 1 per cent per year. A similar assessment in the Federal Republic of Germany yielded a calculated increase in soil concentrations of 0.1 mg/kg^{-1} in 20 to 30 years (Umweltbundesamt, 1981). Taking these observations into consideration, Tjell *et al.* (1983) conclude that at the present Cd load, the average agricultural soils in Europe will increase in Cd content at a rate of 1 to 3 g Cd kg^{-1} year^{-1} in the ploughing layer.

The slow increase in Cd concentrations in soil is relfected in slowly increasing plant concentrations. Although other factors, mainly pH, may have some influence, the indications point to a straightforward relationship between the average Cd concentrations in soil and the average concentrations in plants (Tjell, 1983). Cd concentrations in wheat grain have doubled over the past 50 years in Sweden (Swedish Environmental Protection Board, 1987; Andersson, 1985). In the Federal Republic of Germany it has been pointed out that an increasing fraction of wheat samples have been found to exceed the national regulatory limit for Cd content.

Few attempts have yet been made to establish a connection between the predicted slow increase in soil concentrations of Cd and the human food intake of the metal. All things considered, it may be concluded that an increase of the human load is to be foreseen (Tjell, 1983). It is not possible to predict the actual rate of increase, though.

The kidney is the critical organ for long-term Cd exposure. After long-term relatively low-level exposure to Cd, tubular kidney dysfunction may occur. In some parts of the world, segments of the population have already reached critical concentrations of Cd in the kidneys or are close to critical levels. Even in countries where exposure is low, the margin of safety is small (Friberg *et al.*, 1986).

To protect the human population from the long-term toxic effects of Cd, the total load of Cd on agricultural land must be reduced. To achieve this the regional deposition of Cd as well as the use of Cd-containing fertilizers and sewage sludge must be reduced.

Metals other than Cd have not been included in this evaluation of effects on food uptake. However, a working group organized by the World Health Organization in 1984 considered the risk for health effects of chemicals in sewage sludge applied to land. It was concluded that metals other than Cd were unlikely to cause health problems with normal sludge application (Dean *et al.*, 1985).

The previous conclusion, of course, does not include metals which are predominantly taken up directly from the atmosphere by above-ground plant tissues, as is the case for lead. Pb deposition on agricultural land in rural areas is, however, not supposed to pose a risk for human health. The daily dietary intake of Pb in various countries ranges from mean values of 27 µg per person per day in Sweden to 66 and 77 µg per person per year in Finland and Denmark, respectively. The average dietary intake of lead in the United Kingdom was estimated to be about 110 to 120 µg per day in 1980 (Slorach, 1983). Thus, the daily dietary intake of Pb may be 7 to 25 per cent of the recommended maximum of 400 µg per person per day (equivalent to the provisional tolerable maximum intake of 3 mg per week for an adult) in the normal population (WHO/FAO).

Zn and Cu are essential micronutrients for humans. The dietary intake of Zn and Cu in Sweden, Denmark, Finland and the United Kingdom are on average at the low end of the range considered adequate for adults by a WHO expert group (WHO, 1973) and recommendations by the United States Food and Nutrition Board for male adults (Slorach *et al.*, 1983).

V. CONCLUSIONS

Anthropogenic emissions of heavy metals in Europe, Eurasia and North America contribute to elevated concentrations of these elements in remote areas in the whole northern hemisphere.

The regional concentrations of As, Cd, Cu, Pb, Sb and Zn as measured in recent peat or lake sediments in rural areas are elevated compared to pre-industrial levels, by factors ranging from 5 to 20 or 30 or even more.

The regional atmospheric deposition pattern shows for all metals a large-scale gradient recognizable as influenced by long-range transport from anthropogenic source areas.

The deposition of heavy metals in rural areas increased in many regions up to 1970. Subsequently, this increase has been succeeded by decreases in the concentration levels of many metals. The decreases were most pronounced for Cd and Pb, and were due to lower emissions.

For many metals, the content in topsoils and sediments shows a regional distribution pattern reflecting the atmospheric deposition integrated over several decades. A large-scale gradient is most pronounced for Pb but also evident for Cd, As, V and Sb in soil and Cd, Cu and Zn, for example, in lake sediments.

Effects caused by exposure to heavy metals have been recorded in forest ecosystems and surface waters in the vicinity of point sources. Most studies encompass the synergistic effects of several metals and acid precipitation.

In areas polluted by heavy metals, adverse effects on microbial activity have been reported from a metal concentration in the soil corresponding to about three times the current baseline concentration of comparable soil samples. Improved sampling and measuring techniques would probably allow changes to be detected at an even lower level of pollution. Effects on the bryophyte and lichen flora have been measured at two to three times the current baseline deposition. Vascular plants are usually less influenced by low to intermediate concentrations of heavy metals in soils.

In Scandinavia, regional concentrations of heavy metals in lake or sea water are generally below water-quality guidelines or estimated lowest known effect levels.

There is no evidence of large-scale regional effects of heavy metals in forest ecosystems and surface waters. However, regional concentrations of metals in soils in central Europe are very close to critical concentrations, especially considering the sensitivity of soil biological processes. It should also be emphasized that the effects of prolonged exposure to metals are difficult to measure with existing measuring tools and that reference areas are difficult to find.

In many rural areas, acidification seems to be of greater importance than the regional deposition load of Cd and Zn or the total metal concentration in the soil. Acidification may lead to toxic concentration levels in lakes, and probably in soil and organisms, by mobilization of the metal supply in the soil.

Atmospheric deposition of Cd on agricultural land contributes to the accumulation of Cd in the soil, thereby increasing Cd concentrates in crops, which may be a threat to human health. Cd uptake in vegetation may also lead to elevated concentrations of Cd in wildlife. High concentrations of Cd found for instance in moose liver and kidneys may pose a risk for the moose's health as well as making these organs unfit for human consumption.

The ecological effects on the sea of the atmospheric input of heavy metals have not been evaluated. It has been estimated that the main supply of Pb to the sea is via direct atmospheric deposition on the sea's surface. Atmospheric deposition may account for more than 50 per cent of the Cd and Hg inflow to the Baltic and North Seas. Furthermore, metals originally deposited from the atmosphere on land may reach the sea via streams and rivers. Elevated concentrations of heavy metals have been recorded in surface sediments, for example in the Baltic and in the

Kattegat. As is the case for lakes, high metal concentrations in sediments may constitute a potential risk in terms of effects, but the present state of knowledge is inadequate for an assessment to be made.

Considering the long-term perspective, it must be borne in mind that at the present regional deposition rate, the concentrations of most metals increase in the topsoil and sediment layers. Exceptions are metals such as Cd and Zn that are mainly mobilized when soil pH is low. In many regions, the safety margins are small or may be exceeded. A further increase in metal concentration in the evironment should therefore be avoided. Effects have been observed in the vicinity of point sources. A basic assumption of a balanced soil chemistry should therefore not allow the further accumulation of metals or an increased flow of metals in the soil on a regional basis. This means that emissions of most heavy metals should be reduced.

References

Alderton, D.H.M. Sediments. In MARC report 31, Historical monitoring, p.1-95. Monitoring and Assessment Research Centre of the Scientific Committee on Problems of the Environment, Int. Council of Scientific Unions, London, 1985.

Allen, R.O. and Steinnes (1990). Contributions from long-range atmospheric transport to the heavy metal pollution of surface soils. Proc. Internat. Conf. Ecol. Impact Acid Precipitation, Johs Grefslie Trykkers A/S, Mysen, Norway. Drablos D. and A. Tollan. (eds.) p.102-103.

Andersson, A. (1977). Heavy metals in Swedish soils: on their retention, distribution and amounts. Swedish J. Agric. Res. 7.

Andersson, A. (1985). Trends and annual variations in cadmium concentration in grain of winter wheat. Acta de Agricultura Scandinavia 35: p.339-344.

Balsberg Påhlsson, A-M. (1989). Toxicity of heavy metals (Zn, Cu, Cd, Pb) to vascular plants; a literature review. Water, Air, and Soil Pollution vol. 47: p. 287-319.

Bell, R., C.S. Evans and E.R. Roberts (1988). Decreased incidence of mycorrhizal root tips associated with soil heavy-metal enrichment. Plant and Soil 106: p.143-145.

Bengtsson, G. and L. Tranvik (1989). Critical metal concentrations for forest soil invertebrates. Water, Air, and Soil Pollution vol. 47: p. 381-417.

Bergkvist, B. (1986). Soil solution chemistry and metal budgets of spruce forest ecosystems in Southern Sweden. Water, Air, and Soil Pollution vol.33: p.131-154;

Bergkvist, B., L. Folkeson and D.Berggren (1989). Fluxes of Cu, Zn, Pb, Cd. Cr and Ni in temperate forest ecosystems; a literature review. Water, Air, and Soil Pollution vol. 47: p.217-286.

BMFT (Bundesministerium für Forschung und Technologie) (1985). Umweltforschung zu Waldschäden, 3. Bericht. R. Thierbach, Mühlheim/Ruhr (in German).

Borg, H. (1983). Trace metals in Swedish natural fresh waters. Hydrobiologia 101: p.27-34.

Borg, H. (1987). Trace metals and water chemistry of forest lakes in northern Sweden. Water Research vol. 21, no. 1, p.65-72.

Borg, H. and K. Johansson (1989). Metal fluxes to Swedish forest lakes. Water, Air, and Soil Pollution, vol. 47: p.427-440.

Bååth, E. (1989). Effects of heavy metals in soil on microbial processes and populations (a review). Water, Air, and Soil Pollution, vol. 47: p.335-379.

Bolviken, B. and E. Steinnes (1987). Heavy metal contamination of natural surface soils in Norway from long-range atmospheric transport: Further evidence from analysis of different soil horizons. International Conference on Heavy Metals in the Environment (New Orleans) vol. 1, p.291-293. Eds. S.E. Lindberg and T.C. Hutchinson, Sept. 1987.

Connors, P.G. et al, (1975). Investigations of heavy metals in common tern populations. Can. Field-Nat. 89(2) p.157-162.

Crête, M. et al (1987). Pattern of cadmium contamination in the liver and kidney of moose and white-tailed deer in Quebec. Science of the total environment 66: p.45-53.

Dean, R.B. and M.J. Suess (eds.) (1985). The risk to health of chemicals in sewage sludge applied to land. WHO. Waste Management and Research 3: p.251-278.

Eisler, R. (1985). Cadmium hazards to fish, wildlife, and invertebrates; a synoptic review. U.S. Fish Wildl. Serv. Biol. Rep. 85(1.2). 46.

Eisler, R. (1986). Chromium hazards to fish, wildlife, and invertebrates; a synoptic review. U.S. Fish Wildl. Serv. Biol. Rep. 85(1.6). 60.

Elinder, C.-G. (1981). Early effects of cadmium accumulation in horse kidney cortex. Proc. 3rd Intern. Conf. on Heavy Metals in the Environment (Amsterdam) p.530-533.

EPA. Air Quality Criteria for Lead. June 1986. (Report No. EPA/600/8-83/028 b F).

Frank, A. (1982). Tungmetaller i vilt. Viltnytt 15: p.14-21 (in Swedish).

Frank, A., L. Pettersson and T. Mörner. (1981). Bly- och kadmium-halter i organ fran älg, radjur och hare. Svensk veterinärtidning 33(6): p.151-156 (in Swedish).

Frank, A. (1989). Content of lead and cadmium in liver and kidney from moose and contents of cobalt, copper, manganese and zinc in moose liver in Sweden. Report to the Swedish Environmental Protection Board (in Swedish).

Friberg, L. et al. (eds.) (1986). Cadmium and health; a toxicological and epidemiological appraisal. CRC Press, Inc. Boca Raton, Florida.

Froslie, A. et al. (1984). Levels of trace elements in liver from Norwegian moose, reindeer and red deer in relation to atmospheric deposition. Acta vet. scand 25: p.333-345: 1984.

Förstner, U and G. Wittman (1979). Metal pollution in the aquatic environment. Springer, Berlin.

Glooschenko, V. et al (1987). Cadmium levels in Ontario moose and the implications for human resource users. Proc. Int. Conf. Heavy metals in the Environment. (New Orleans) vol.2: p.42-44: Sept. 1987.

Hatum, O.O., E. Steinnes and B. Bolviken (1987). Regional differences and temporal trends in heavy metal deposition from the atmosphere studied by analysis of ombrotrophic peat. International Conference on Heavy Metals in the Environment vol. 1: p.201-203. Eds. S.E. Lindberg and T.C. Hutchinson, New Orleans: Sept. 1987.

Heinrichs, H. and R. Mayer (1980). The role of forest vegetation in the biogeochemical cycle of heavy metals. J. Environm. Qual. 9: p.111-118.

Heinrichs, H. et al (1985). Hydrochemie der Quellen und kleineren Züflüsse der Sösetalsperre (Harz) in Abhängigkeit vom Untergrund. Manuscript (in German) cited in Materialien 4187, Umweltbundesamt.

Holm, J. (1979). Blei-, Cadmium- und Arsengehalte in Fleisch und Organproben von Wild aus unterschiedlich schadmetallbelasteten Regionen. Fleischwirtschaft 59(9): p.1345-1349: 1979 (in German).

Holt, G., A. Froslie and G. Norheim (1978). Blyforgiftning hos norske svommefugler (Lead poisoning in Norwegian water fowl). Nord. Vet.-Med. 30: p.380-386 (in Norwegian).

Jenkins, D.W. (1980). Biological monitoring of toxic trace metals: volume 2. Toxic trace metals in plants and animals of the world. U.S. Environmental Protection Agency - Las Vegas, NV. (EPA-600/3-80-090).

Johansson, K. (1989). Metals in sediment of lakes in northern Sweden. Water, Air, and Soil Pollution vol. 47: p.441-455.

Kabata-Pendias, A. and H. Pendias (1984). Trace elements in soils and plants. CRC Press, Inc. Boca Raton, Florida.

Lamersdorf, N. (1988). Verteilung and Akkumulation von Spurenstoffen in Waldökosystemen. Berichte des Forschungszentrums Waldökosysteme/Waldsterben, Reihe A, Bd 36 (in German).

Lannefors, H., H.-C. Hansson and L. Granat (1983). Background aerosol composition in southern Sweden - 14 micro and macro constitutents measured in seven particle size intervals at one site during one year. Atm. Environment, 17: p.87-101.

Ledin, A., et al (1989). Background concentration ranges of heavy metals in Swedish groundwaters from crystalline rocks; A review. Water, Air, and Soil Pollution vol. 47: p.419-426.

Ledin, A., et al. (1989). Heavy metals in groundwaters. Report to the Swedish Environmental Protection Board.

Lithner, G. (1989). Some fundamental relationships between metal toxicity in fresh water, intrinsic properties and background levels. Accepted for publication in Science of the Total Environment.

Lutz, W. (1985). Ergebnisse der Untersuchungen von Rehen (Capreolus capreolus L.) und Hasen (Lepus europaeus Pallas) auf Schwermetalle und chlorierte Kohlenwasserstoffe in Nordrhein-Westfalen Z. Jagdwiss 31: p.153-175 (in German).

Martinsson, B.G., H.-C. Hansson and H.O. Lannefors (1984). Southern Scandinavian aerosol composition and elemental size distribution characteristics dependence on air-mass history. Atmospheric Environment 18: p.2167-2182.

Mattsson, P., L. Albanus and A. Frank (1981). Kadmium och vissa andra metaller i lever och njure fran älg. Var föda 33: p.335-345 (in Swedish).

Mayer, R. (1985). Mobilisierung von Aluminium und Schwermetallen in Bodenbereich durch Säurebildner. Manuscript to Umweltbundesamt (Berlin) cited in Materialien 4/87 (in German).

Monitor (1987). The occurrence and turnover of heavy metals in the environment (in Swedish).

Muller, P. (1985). Cadmium-Konzentrationen bei Rehpopulationen (*Capreolus capreolus*) und deren Futterpflanzen. Z. Jagdwiss 31: p.146-153 (in German).

Nyholm, N.E.I. (1987). Bio-indication of industrial emissions of heavy metals by means of insectivorous birds. Proc. Int. Conf. Heavy Metals in the Environment (New Orleans) vol. 2: p.45-47: Sept. 1987.

Pacyna, J.M. (1986). Emission factors of atmospheric elements. In: Toxic metals in the atmosphere. Edited by J.O. Nriagu and C.J. Davidson. Wiley Sons, Inc.

Pacyna, J.M. (1987). Source-receptor relationships for atmospheric trace elements in Europe. In: Acid precipitation. D.C. Adriano, W. Salomons (eds). Springer Verlag, N.Y. (in press).

Pacyna, J.M. et al. (1989). Modelling of long-range transport of trace elements; a case-study. Paper accepted for publication in Atmospheric Environment.

Pacyna, J.M. and B. Ottar (1985). Transport and chemical composition of the summer aerosol in the Norwegian Arctic. Atmospheric Environment vol. 19, no. 12: p.2109-2120.

Pacyna, J.M., A. Semb and J.E. Hanssen (1984). Emission and long-range transport of trace elements in Europe. Tellus 36 B.: p.163-178.

Pacyna, J.M., V. Vitols and J.E. Hanssen (1984). Size-differentiated composition of the Arctic aerosol at Ny-Alesund, Spitsbergen. Atmospheric Environment vol. 18 no. 11: p.2447-2459.

Pacyna, J.M., A. Semb and J.E. Hanssen (1984). Emission and long-range transport of trace elements in Europe. Tellus 36 B.: p.163-178.

Pacyna, J.M., V. Vitols and J.E. Hanssen 1984). Size-differentiated composition of the Arctic aerosol at Ny-Alesund, Spitsbergen. Atmospheric Environment vol. 18 no. 11: p.2447-2459.

Ros, J.P.M. and W. Slooff (eds.) (1988). Integrated criteria document Cadmium. National Institute of Public Health and Environmental Protection, Bilthoven. Report no. 758476004.

Ross, H.B. (1987. Trace metals in precipitation in Sweden. Water, Air and Soil Pollution vol. 36: p.349-363.

Rühling, A. et al. Survey of atmospheric heavy metal deposition monitored by moss analysis. Report prepared for The Steering Body for Environmental Monitoring. The Nordic Council of Ministers. (NORD 1987:21).

Scheuhammer, A.M. (1987). The chronic toxicity of cadmium, mercury, and lead in birds; a review. Environm. Poll. 46: p.263-295: 1987.

Sileo, L. and W.N. Beyer (1984) Heavy metals in white-tailed deer living near a zink smelter in Pennsylvania. Journal of Wildlife Diseases vol. 21, no. 3: July 1985.

Slorach, S. et al. (1983). Intake of lead, cadmium and certain other metals via a typical Swedish weekly diet. Report from the National Swedish Food Administration vol. 35, supplement 1.

Steinnes, E.(1987). Impact of long-range atmospheric transport of heavy metals to the terrestrial environment in Norway. In: Lead, mercury, cadmium and arsenic in the environment. Edited by T.C. Hutchinson and K.M. Meema. SCOPE, John Wiley Sons Ltd.

Steinnes, E. and E. Breivik (1987). Micropollutants in the terrestrial environment in Norway. SFT Report no. 83 (Oslo) (in Norwegian).

Swedish Environmental Protection Board (1987). Cadmium in the environment. Report no. 3317 (in Swedish).

Tataruch, F. and K. Onderscheka (1982). Das freilebende Tier als Indikator für die Umweltbelastung mit Schwermetallen und Pestiziden. Wien. Tierärztl. Mschr. 69. Jahrgang Heft 10/1982: p.280-282 (in German).

Tjell, J.C. and T.H. Christensen (1985). Evidence of increasing cadmium contents of agricultural soils. Proceedings from International Conference on Heavy Metals in the Environment (Athens) vol.2: p.391-393: September 1985.

Tjell, J.C., T.H. Christensen and F. Bro-Rasmussen (1983). Cadmium in soils and terrestrial biota with emphasis on the Danish situation. Ecotoxicology and Environmental Safety 7: p.122-140.

Tyler, G. (1989). Bryophytes and heavy metals; a literature review. Proc. Linnaean Soc. (in press).

Tyler, G. (1989). Uptake, retention and toxicity of heavy metals in lichens; a brief review. Water, Air and Soil Pollution vol. 47: p.321-333.

Tyler, G. *et al.* (1989). Heavy-metal ecology of terrestrial plants, mico-organisms and invertebrates; a review. Water, Air and Soil Pollution vol. 47: p. 189-215.

UBA (1981). Cadmium-Bericht. Umweltbundesamt, Berlin 1/81 (in German).

Ulrich, B. (1984). Deposition von Säure und Schwermetallen aus Luftverunreinigungen und ihre Auswirkungen in Waldökosystemen. In: Metalle in der Umwelt. Verteilung, Analytik und biologische Relevanz. Herausgegeben von Ernest Merian, Verlag Chemie, GmbH, D-6940 Weinheim (in German): 1984.

Vahter, M. and S. Slorach (eds). Integrated exposure monitoring of lead and cadmium. An international pilot study within the UNEP/WHO Human Exposure Assessment Location. HEAL Project. Draft 1988-11-21 from the Technical Coordinating Centre, Stockholm.

Wagner, G. and P. Müller (1979). Fichten als "Bioindikatoren" für die Immissionsbelastung urbaner Okosysteme unter besonderer Berücksichtigung von Schwermetallen. Verhandlungen der Gesellschaft für Okologie, Münster 1978, Band VII, 307-314 (in German).

WHO (1972). Report of the joint FAO/WHO expert committee on food additives, WHO Food Additives Series no. 4. World Health Organization, Geneva.

Woolf, A. *et al.* (1982). Metals in livers of whitetailed deer in Illinois, USA. Bull. Environm. Contam. Toxicol. 28(2): p.189-194.

Part FIVE

ECONOMIC AND COST IMPACT OF AIR POLLUTION ABATEMENT STRATEGIES

Economic and cost impact analyses form an essential part of the overall economic evaluation of alternative strategies for the abatement of sulphur oxides (SO_x) and nitrogen oxides (NO_x) emissions.

Some countries are in the process of developing models on economic and cost impacts, but cannot yet provide final results. Other countries are able to provide data but there are significant differences in the kind of data contained in the national reports. After an overview of the wide spectrum of the economic effects of air pollution abatement measures, the present survey provides specific information as reported by Austria, Finland, France, the Federal Republic of Germany, the Netherlands, Poland, the Union of Soviet Socialist Republics, and the United Kingdom.

Cost-impact data on pollution-reduction expenditures need to be assessed on the basis of information on environmental protection policies, economic policies and characteristics of the structure of industry. Differences in pollution abatement options also relate to specifics of energy demand, energy mix, quality of fuel used, specific supply/demand conditions for raw materials, export/import structures and price and demand elasticities. The scarcity of such information in some countries can create difficulties for the economic evaluation of emission reduction scenarios for the longer-term perspective, that is, up to the year 2005.

Further studies in the area of economic and cost impact analyses of pollution control should also make use of other information readily available. Annual expenditures by industry/Governments on pollution control are recorded in national statistics while in most countries projections on expenditures are also available.

Chapter 1: ECONOMIC IMPACT ANALYSIS

The economic impact assessment of air pollution abatement policies has different implications according to the short-term or long-term perspectives. For short-term impacts, the results vary depending on the specific structure and performance of economies, on the age of plants and the possibilities for short-term structural change within a branch of industry as well as national economies. Indicators for economic impact include the effects on the size and composition of gross domestic product (GDP)/net material product (NMP), employment levels, consumer prices, investment by Governments and industry, etc.

I. EFFECTS ON GDP/NMP

Assessments of the effects on GDP/NMP differ in both the short-term and long-term perspectives. In principle, an initial growth of GDP may be assumed owing to more investments in pollution control.[1] In addition to the rise in capital investment, there are positive employment effects. Multiplier and accelerator effects lead to higher growth rates. For the longer-term outlook, assessments range from a negative impact on GDP to a positive impact, depending on the country.[2] As pollution-control investments are reduced or cease (depending on the time-frame of different countries for the implementation of policies), the positive impact on GDP likewise decreases. Economies with fully utilized labour and production capacities react differently to economies with under-utilized labour and production capacities. Investment for pollution control in the latter case will lead to economic growth, *inter alia*, increasing the demand for employment, without putting pressure on other production sectors.[3] Another important factor in terms of economic effects is the technology chosen for pollution control. While add-on technologies increase production costs without increasing the capacity of plants, integrated technologies may contribute significantly to production growth and decreased costs in the long term as raw material and energy inputs decrease.

In principle, the effect of pollution control policies on GDP/NMP is in most cases not of a major order of magnitude. The results of a Norwegian general equilibrium growth model predicted a loss in GDP of between 0.008 per cent to 0.02 per cent for the year 2000 owing to control policy, depending on the policy.[4] According to a study on macro-economic impacts in the EEC, positive impacts range from +0.17 per cent to +0.06 per cent for the period 1988 to 1993. For the period 1994 to 1997, the range spans from -0.21 to +0.05.[5] According to a study on the effectiveness of the protection of the atmosphere in the USSR, the capital investments for protection of the atmosphere under the Tenth Five-year Plan represented less than 0.4 per cent of total capital investment in industry.[6]

Improved air quality may alone have a positive impact on growth of GDP/NMP. The Norwegian model mentioned above calculated that one hour less sick-leave per employee per year was enough to compensate for any loss in GDP attributable to pollution control.[7] Improved environmental quality may also lead to increased growth opportunities for certain industries, like expansion in tourism, forestry and agricultural sectors.

Conventional calculations of GDP/NMP do not take into account the majority of costs associated with damage by air pollution simply because externalities are not normally accounted for in national accounts. Through the internalization of such external costs true social costs may be more accurately reflected.

II. EFFECTS ON EMPLOYMENT

Pollution control policies have both a direct and an indirect impact on employment. It may be positive or negative, depending on the parameters indicated above with reference to effects on GDP/NMP. Direct positive effects include demand for labour in the sectors of industry producing goods and services which control pollution; indirect positive effects stem from additional demand for intermediate goods and services. Induced positive effects result from multiplier-effects. Direct negative effects result from plant closures owing to pollution control measures. Indirect and induced negative effects reflect changes in the demand for intermediate goods and services. Regional and sectoral effects

will of course be considerably larger than overall effects.

Impact on employment levels differs according to the short-term and the long-term perspectives. In the short term a positive impact is more likely owing to the relatively heavy investment programmes; in the long term, the result may possibly be a decline in employment, as price and income effects are felt.[8] The impact on employment in the longer-term perspective is, however, considered to be of a minor magnitude, and net positive effects are considered more likely to emerge than net negative effects.[9] Data for the Federal Republic of Germany may serve as an example for the order of magnitude of positive employment effects. The total employed labour force amounted in 1985 to 25 million. The predicted effects on employment of the Ordinance on Large Combustion Installations are forecast as follows. The employment effects of flue-gas treatment required by the Ordinance to be implemented by 1993 will amount in the construction stage to an estimated 300,000 work years with respect to investments and to about 27,000 jobs per year with regard to operation and maintenance.[10] This amounts to 0.108 per cent of the total labour force for the operation and maintenance of emission control alone. A forecast of negative effects from plant closure because of environmental policies as a whole indicates a yearly average of 0.015 per cent to 0.04 per cent.[11] However, these figures cover the whole range of environmental protection measures while negative effects on employment levels owing to air pollution control represent only a part thereof. In the overall analysis, the impact on employment is considered positive in the initial stage of pollution control measures, and possible negative effects in the long term will be either minor or even counter-balanced by additional short-term positive effects induced by further pollution control measures.

III. EFFECTS ON PRICES

Effects on prices will differ between "sheltered" and "exposed" sectors, between subsidized and non-subsidized industries and between the use of added-on and integrated technologies. Sheltered industries, not facing foreign competition, can pass on pollution control costs, while exposed industries may not be in a position to do so. Subsidized industries will not incur increased costs, at least not fully. Subsidies will, however, have effects on the expenditure side of government budgets. In the case of integrated pollution control technologies, it is difficult to identify the specific portion of the investment attributable to pollution control, and expenditure for pollution control may not lead to proportionate cost increases because productivity may increase.

Direct cost effects are in general easily identifiable. They will be observed mostly in the primary production sector, for example in such industries as paper, chemicals, and steel refineries. Indirect cost effects, that is, purchases of intermediate products of the output from the above-mentioned sectors, will be lower but are harder to quantify. In general, input-output statistics can serve as a yardstick to estimate such indirect cost/price effects.

Overall, price effects seem not to be of a major magnitude. For instance, cost effects for air-pollution control for Austrian industry as a whole have been estimated at 0.37 per cent of production value (overall cost effects of 0.84 per cent for total environmental protection).[12] Corresponding figures for the Tenth Five-year Plan in the USSR are 0.4 per cent of capital investment.[13] The study on the macro-economic impact of the EEC directive for large combustion plants also recorded only slight rises in consumer prices.[14] In the Federal Republic of Germany the impact of the Ordinance on Large Combustion Installations has been calculated as resulting in an increase in production costs of 0.02 DM/kwh for electricity generation in plants with flue-gas treatment. For total electricity generation this corresponds to a price increase of 0.01 DM/kwh.[15] For some sectors or for specific regions or individual plants, pollution control costs may represent a heavier burden.

Positive impacts of pollution control measures on prices can result from innovations which in the long-run might have price-decreasing effects. Positive impacts can also be induced by a more efficient use of capacities. These factors will be discussed in a later chapter.

IV. ENERGY DEMAND PROJECTIONS

In a number of countries energy policies include, or even focus on, energy conservation. Already during the past decade, growth of energy use was not necessarily proportionally linked to production growth. At least until the latest fall in oil prices, the elasticity of energy demand with respect to output growth was smaller than one in most economies. A more rational use of energy and changes in the pattern of energy consumption are efficient means for reducing emissions. Projected changes in energy systems include changes from oil to electricity (e.g. to hydro power), use of waste heat (district heating), development and modification of industrial processes (recirculation and reutilization).

Such policies allow significant reductions of emissions and provide more cost-effective means for the production process and the overall use of energy. For achieving environmental policy goals, changes in the energy system are considered by some countries as at least as efficient as strict standards for emissions.[16]

V. EFFECTS ON INDUSTRIAL STRUCTURE

Pollution control measures can have a considerable positive impact on the industrial structure of countries and on the performance of individual plants. Research and development as well as investment in low-pollution techologies usually lower costs per unit of output in the long run besides reducing total and average emission levels. Overall, emission standards can provoke an acceleration of the replacement of old plants - depending on the strictness of standards - with modern plants, in the energy-intensive primary production industry. Clean technologies may also provide for a reduction in investment cost (in 10 per cent of cases) and operating costs (in 70 per cent of cases) in comparison with earlier processes, mainly because of energy and raw-material savings.[17] "Learning-by-doing" effects will lead to lower installation and operating costs.[18] Industries which previously made low investments in technology may experience problems with the implementation of pollution control policies. More stringent emission standards may improve their economic performance and production capacity through the introduction of new technologies.[19]

Structural change in some economies, a change which accelerated during the late 1970s, has in some cases led to a stabilization of emission levels but not to significant reductions. In the short term, a structural shift of economies from emission-intensive to less-polluting sectors does not seem feasible. Add-on technologies for controlling emissions will for some time to come still be needed for supplementing the change from emission-intensive production processes to low-emission production technologies and the substitution of fuels. In the long-term development, the structural change of economies may lead to the replacement of emission-intensive products with imports or low-emission production processes.[20] Moreover, shifts from the primary production sector to the secondary sector and the service sector may also significantly reduce emissions. However, it should not be overlooked that the secondary and tertiary sectors are not "pollution-free".

Technological innovations may be accelerated by emission standards. Technological spin-offs may, in addition, lead to efficiency increases of production processes and energy savings while decreasing raw-material consumption. Important factors of the positive effect of emission standards on structural changes and innovation include clear time-frames for pollution control policies, a certain flexibility for technical measures, definition of long-term goals, sufficient provision of information to industries, consultations with industries, strict enforcement of standards, definition of standards, subsidies, etc.[21]

In general, emission standards can have positive effects on technological and hence on structural change if the planning process is undertaken in co-operation with industries and when clear time-frames and goals are stated.

VI. EFFECTS ON INTERNATIONAL TRADE/COMPETITIVENESS

In the international context, a country mainly encounters problems owing to pollution control measures if similar measures are not adopted by competitors. International competitiveness and thus trade balances may be affected by control-induced price increases. Exports may decrease and imports increase on account of purchases of pollution control equipment. The early development of industries producing emission control and monitoring technology will, however, result in favourable effects on the international competitiveness of industries (see also the above chapter on the effects on industrial structure). The international flow of production factors such as capital, influencing the location of firms, is not determined by pollution control policies. Lack of emission standards does not have much influence on industries in their decisions concerning the location of new plants within the region.[22] Although the impact of pollution control measures does not seem of major magnitude compared with other factors (labour costs, raw-material cost, energy cost, competitiveness of production process technologies) concerted international action for pollution control would stabilize international competitiveness and decrease any possible negative effects on individual countries taking a lead position in emission control.

Chapter 2: COST IMPACT ANALYSIS

The information received for cost-impact analysis of different SO_x abatement strategies does not allow a concise regional assessment. Contributions varied both in length and in aggregation of information. A uniform presentation has not been attempted, as the more disaggregated data provided may provide valuable examples of cost-impact analysis for countries currently undertaking this exercise.

I. EXPENDITURE ON AIR POLLUTION CONTROL IN AUSTRIA

Expenditure by industry on air pollution abatement in Austria in the period 1974 to 1977 amounted to 30 per cent of total expenditure on environmental protection. In the period 1982 to 1986 this ratio grew to 43.3 per cent and is estimated for the period 1987 to 1990 at 45.4 per cent, the biggest expenditure share of all sectors of environmental protection. Total costs for the period 1980 to 1990 are presented in table 8 in millions of Austrian schillings.

Investments by the electricity production sector for the years 1982 to 1984 came to a yearly average of 1,660 million Austrian schillings.[25] Information on operation and maintenance is not yet available for this sector. The estimated reduction of SO_2 emissions will reach 90 per cent; NO_x abatement is calculated at between 40 and 65 per cent.

Table 8

Total costs of air pollution control for industry in Austria (annual average)[24]

	1980-81	1982-84	1985-86	1987-90
Investment	712.4	896.8	2 996.8	2 732.9
Operation and maintenance	896.8	1 403.4	1 729.7	1 741.9
Total cost	1 609.2	2 300.2	4 726.5	4 474.8

II. EXPENDITURE ON AIR POLLUTION CONTROL IN FINLAND

An input-output-based steady-state growth model has been developed by the University of Oulu, but the results of cost-impact and economic impact analyses of pollution control are not yet available. However, information is available on projected emission reductions and the cost thereof, mainly in the Sulphur Commission report.[26] The considerable reduction in 1993 of the 1980 SO_2 emission levels in Finland is influenced by changes in the energy production sector and the structure of industries.

It has been estimated that, as a consequence of structural change and clearly predictable measures aimed at protecting the quality of the air, emissions would range from 280,000 to 400,000 tonnes in 1993, compared with 584,000 tonnes in 1980. Emissions will undergo a relative decrease ranging from 30 to 50 per cent.

The costs arising in conjunction with these measures may be estimated on the basis of surveys. Depending on the nature of the measures taken, they range from FIM 3,000 to FIM 12,000 per tonne of sulphur removed. If it was necessary to reduce emissions of sulphur dioxide by 100,000 tonnes annually, for example, the annual expenses would range from FIM 200-600 million, depending on the means used.

III. EXPENDITURE ON AIR POLLUTION CONTROL IN FRANCE

SO$_2$ emissions in France dropped by an annual average of 6.4 per cent between 1973 and 1985, with all sectors of industry contributing to the reduction. NO$_x$ emissions reached their maximum level in 1979. Since then they have been steadily diminishing at an average rate of 2.6 per cent per year. Only the transportation sector does not contribute to NO$_x$ reductions (2.2 per cent average yearly increase since 1973). Transport contributed 72 per cent of NO$_x$ emissions in 1985. The expenditures on air pollution control for industry in France are shown in table 9.

Table 9

Costs of air pollution control for industry in France for the years
1978-1984 (in millions of French francs (1984 level)[27]

	1978	1982	1983	1984
Investment	1 830	1 600	1 460	1 600
Operation and maintenance	2 400	2 800	2 850	2 900
Total cost	4 230	4 400	4 310	4 500

IV. EXPENDITURE ON AIR POLLUTION CONTROL IN THE FEDERAL REPUBLIC OF GERMANY

A. Regulation and action

In the late 1970s, preparatory work was initiated in the Federal Republic of Germany for setting strict standards for the emission of SO$_2$ and NO$_x$ from combustion plants. Such emission standards were enacted on 1 July 1983 with the Ordinance on Large Combustion Plants (*Grossfeuerungsanlagen-Verordnung*). For nearly all fossil-fuelled power plants, i.e, plants with a thermal rating of more than 300 MW, the Ordinance stipulates an SO$_2$ emission standard of 400 mg/m^3 and an SO$_2$ emission rate of less than 15 per cent. These emission standards took immediate effect for all new plants. Existing plants have had to comply with these standards since 1 July 1988 following a transitional period which had been allowed for planning, licensing and installation. In 1984, the regulations for NO$_x$ were adapted to the state-of-the-art technology, stipulating NO$_x$ emission standards of 200 mg/m^3 for coal-fired, 150 mg/m^3 for oil-fired, and 100 mg/m^3 for gas-fired plants. These standards likewise took immediate effect for new plants, while for existing plants a 1990 deadline was stipulated, but without a precise date being set.

Table 10 gives an overview of the SO$_2$ and NO$_x$ emission standards. Table 11 shows some important data on electricity supply in the Federal Republic of Germany.

B. De-SO$_x$ programme at power plants

Until 30 June 1988, nearly all coal-fired power plants in operation (28,000 MW$_e$ hard coal; 11,000 MW$_e$ lignite) had been retrofitted with flue gas desulphurization (FGD) plants. Most oil-fired plants were switched to low-sulphur fuels.

In the utilities sector, some 165 FGD plants with a flue-gas volume of 135 million m^3/h have been installed and put into operation at 72 power plant sites in the Federal Republic of Germany. Eighty-seven per cent of the capacity of these plants use lime/limestone scrubbers whose desulphurization product is gypsum. Seven per cent are dry-sorption and spray-dryer plants from which a mixture of calcium sulphate, calcium sulphite and other substances result as the final product. The remaining capacity is shared by regenerative processes, such as the Wellman-Lord process and the process developed by Bergbau-Forschung with their marketable products sulphur and sulphuric acid, and the Walther process. Figure 1 shows the development in capacity of desulphurization plants.

Modern FGD plants reflect state-of-the-art control technology based on more than 20 years of development work. The lime and limestone scrubbers which are predominantly used are cost-effective, reliable, relatively easy to manage, and have a high desulphurization efficiency. The sorbents are inexpensive and can be obtained without any transportation problems. The desulphurization product gypsum (approximately 3.3 million tonnes per annum) can be used as a substitute for natural gypsum in its conventional areas of use (e.g. building plaster, gypsum wallboards, setting retarder in cement). In addition, there is a high potential for new usage, e.g. as a component of mining mortar and in the manufacture of gypsum chipboard. Operators of coal-fired power plants and the gypsum industry have concluded long-term delivery and acceptance contracts. The gypsum from lignite-fired power plants (1 million tonnes per annum), together with fly and boiler ash as well as FGD plant effluent, is still deposited in open-cast mines.

Table 10

Emission standards for sulphur and nitrogen oxides as stipulated in
the Ordinance on Large Combustion Plants and by the Conference of the Federal
and Länder Environment Ministers of 5 April 1984

Fuel	Thermal rating	Sulphur dioxide[a] (as SO_2)	Nitrogen oxides[b] (as NO_2)	O_2 reference value (dry, 1013 mbar, O C)
Solid	> 300 MW	400 mg/m³ and emission rate of less than 15 per cent	200 mg/m³	
	100 to 300 MW	2000 mg/m³ and emission rate of less than 40 per cent	400 mg/m³	5 per cent wet bed 6 per cent dry bed 9 per cent grid firing
	50 to 100 MW	2000 mg/m³ [c]		
Liquid	> 300 MW	Gasoil or 400 mg/m³ and emission rate of less than 15 per cent	150 mg/m³	
	100 to 300 MW	Gasoil or 1700 mg/m³ and emission rate of less than 40 per cent		3 per cent
	50 to 100 MW	1700 mg/m³	300 mg/m³	
Gaseous	> 300 MW	35 mg/m³	100 mg/m³	
		5 mg/m³ liquified gas		3 per cent
	100 to 300 MW	100 mg/m³ coke-oven gas	200 mg/m³	

a/ Since 1 July 1988, new plants with a residual useful life of unlimited duration (> 30,000 h) have had to comply with the same requirements as for new plants. Less stringent requirements for existing plants with a residual useful life of limited duration will only be effective until 1 April 1993; after that date, the same requirements as for new plants will apply.
b/ Existing plants with a residual useful life of unlimited duration will have to comply with the following requirements as soon as possible (1990 at the latest): > 300 MW, as for new plants; < 300 MW: 650 mg/m³ or 1,300 mg/m³ for wet bottom boilers (solid fuels); 450 mg/m³ (liquid fuels); 350 mg/m³ (gaseous fuels).
c/ Fluidized-bed combustion: 400 mg/m³, or a maximum emission rate of 25 per cent.

Table 11

Power plant capacity, gross electricity production and rnergy input

	Capacity MW	Operating hours h/a	Gross electricity production GWh	Energy Input 1000 TCE
Hydro	6 630	2 900	19 227	6 049
Nuclear	23 863	6 000	143 178	47 095
Lignite	13 760	6 700	92 192	32 952
Hardcoal	32 797	3 934	122 944	38 880
Gas	12 489	1 784	31 541	9 289
Oil	8 548	1 448	9 198	2 561
Total	98 087		418 280[a]	136 826

a/ 355 TWh thereof generated in public power plants.

Figure 1
FGD and SCR capacity at power plants
in the Federal Republic of Germany

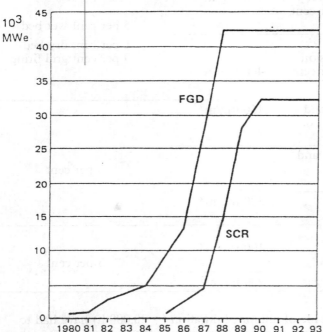

Figure 2
The trend of annual SO_2 and NO_x emissions
in the Federal Republic of Germany

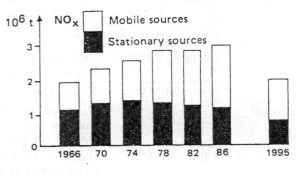

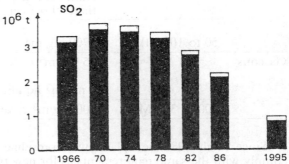

C. De-NOx programme at power plants

Considerable progress has also been made in the reduction of NO_x emissions from power plants. To a great extent, retrofitting with primary measures had already been completed in 1988. Except for a few plants, all oil-, gas- and lignite-fired plants, which *per se* have lower NO_x emissions owing to their specific construction and fuels, are able to comply with the emission standards without flue-gas cleaning. Coal-fired power plants, however, require flue-gas cleaning

in any case. The process exclusively employed is selective catalytic reduction (SCR process) with ammonia. The reactor is placed either directly behind the boiler (high dust system) or downstream from the FGD plant (tail-gas system). The retrofitting of large combustion plants with NO_x flue-gas cleaning has made rapid progress (figure 1) since the first plants went into operation in 1985 on a commercial scale (unit 5 at Altback/Deizisau of the Neckarwerke Elektrizitätsversorgung AG; VEBA Kraftwerke Ruhr AG in Buer). At the end of 1988, plants with a total capacity of 12,000 MW$_e$ were in operation.

D. Emission reductions

A drastic reduction of SO$_2$ and NO$_x$ emissions is achieved as a result of the Ordinance on Large Combustion Plants. Compared to 1983 levels, SO$_2$ emissions from power plants were reduced by 65 per cent to approximately 0.7 million t/a in 1988 and will be reduced further by a total of 80 per cent to approximately 0.4 million t/a once the Ordinance takes full effect in 1993. Up to 1988, the nitric oxide emissions had been reduced by 38 per cent to 0.6 million tonnes, measured against 1983 levels, and will have dropped by 74 per cent to 0.25 million tonnes by the early 1990s. Figure 2 shows the trend of SO$_2$ and NO$_x$ emissions broken down into important source sectors.

E. Investment

According to a survey conducted by the Federation of Electric Power Companies in the Federal Republic of Germany (VDEW), public utilities have made investments amounting to DM 14.3 billion for FGD plants with a total capacity of some 38,000 MW$_e$. For the denitrification of power plants, that means that for primary measures and for approximately 33,000 MW$_e$ of SCR plants, investments of approximately DM 7 billion are expected. This is in line with earlier estimates conducted by the Federal Environmental Agency in 1983/1984 when the Ordinance

went into effect, which set the total expenditure for desulphurization at DM 13 billion and about half of that amount for denitrification.[28, 29]

Figure 3 shows the average investments for gas cleaning at coal-fired power plants as a function of the thermal rating (MW) with respect to the lime/limestone process. Curve A represents the actual investments for retrofit plants, whereas curve B reflects manufacturer calculations for new plants. The survey data approximated in the DEW-FGD curve scatter widely. This is mainly owing to the different site-specific retrofit conditions, such as construction work that needs to be done on the existing power plant in order to make room for the FGD plant or to incorporate it into the power plant, costly foundations, and longer and more complex flue-gas ducts. Experts estimate the additional expenditure for FGD retrofit plants at 30 per cent of the investment required for new plants. A comparison of the two curves in figure 3 (A and B) seems to confirm a retrofit factor of 30 per cent.

The investment for SCR plants (curve C) which is likewise presented in figure 3 refers only to new plants not equipped with catalysts. A corresponding curve for retrofit plants is not yet available. The six SCR high-dust retrofit plants for coal-fired dry-bottom furnaces which were already in operation in 1988 required additional investments of 50 per cent on average.

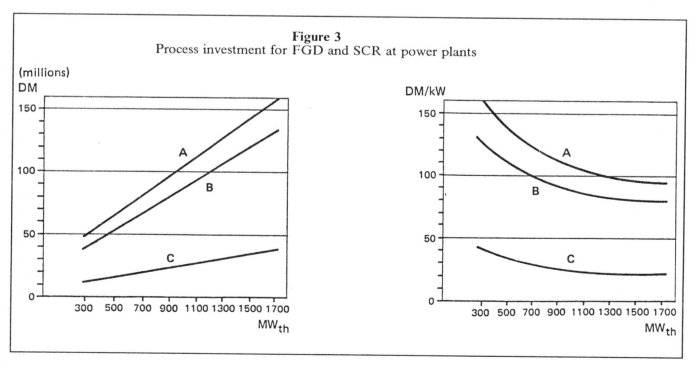

Figure 3
Process investment for FGD and SCR at power plants

According to rough estimates, the approximately DM 22 billion flue-gas cleaning programme has

had a macro-economic impact on production amounting to nearly DM 60 billion, thus safeguarding some 300,000 jobs (man years) at construction sites and suppliers. The operation of the plants which is highly automated and not very labour-intensive has resulted in the creation of approximately 1,000 jobs.

F. Annual costs

According to their different characteristics, the annual costs for flue-gas cleaning can be divided into capital-dependent fixed costs and operation-related variable costs, such as energy, sorbents, reducing agents, and catalysts. Important variables influencing the costs are the flue-gas volume to be treated, the amount of pollutants to be removed, and the annual operating hours.

G. Fixed costs

Fixed costs include depreciation, interest, staff, maintenance, repairs, taxes, insurance, and overheads. These costs can be expressed as a percentage of the investment. They may vary considerably, depending on the particular plant in question. An average value of 18 per cent of the initial investment is considered realistic for the situation in the Federal Republic of Germany.

1. Energy

In modern flue-gas cleaning plants, the flue gas is reheated without the use of additional energy by means of regenerative heat exchangers. The use of additional energy is merely necessary in cases where, owing to a lack of space or for operational reasons, the tail-gas option of the SCR process was chosen to remove NO_x from the flue gas. The additional energy required here to reheat the flue gas by about 50° C is approximately 300 kJ/kWh. The electrical energy demand of fans and pumps for the operation of FGD and SCR plants amounts to approximately 1.5 per cent of the plant capacity; it may, however, be twice as high in the case of retrofit plants, because of longer flue gas channels.

2. Sorbents/Reducing agent

Limestone ($CaCO_3$) has become the prevalent sorbent in the lime scrubbing process. It is used in a stoichiometric ratio to SO_2 (approximately 8 grams of $CaCO_3$ per kWh in the case of coal with a sulphur content of 1 per cent). Limestone is offered at DM 40 per tonne. The limestone

quantitites required for the de-SO_2 programme amount to some 2 million tonnes annually. The water demand of a lime/limestone scrubber is approximately 0.12 litre/kWh. The ammonia consumption of the SCR process is proportionate to the NO_x volume to be reduced. For example, the collection of 800 mg of NO_x requires the use of 1 gram of NH_3, which is sold for DM 500 per tonne. Around 200,000 tonnes of NH_3 per year are needed for the entire de-NO_x programme.

3. Catalysts

In addition to TiO_2 catalysts which are used predominantly, iron oxide/chromium oxide catalysts, molecular sieves and activated coke are used to a minor extent to reduce NO_x. When installing a TiO_2 catalyst for the first time, a volume of approximately 1 m³/MW is needed. Since operational experience has been quite positive (low dust accumulation, low deactivation), the catalyst is currently assumed to have a service life of more than five years. The price for the catalyst has dropped by more than 50 per cent since 1985 and now stands at DM 20 000/m³. It is estimated that, in the 1990s, a catalyst volume of approximately 5,000 m³ will have to be replaced annually for all SCR plants.

H. Costs for electricity generation

The additional costs for electricity generation arising from the SO_2 and NO_x emission reduction measures lie basically within a range of 0.015 and 0.035 DM/kWh, depending on the circumstantial conditions on site. The cost example presented in figure 4 has been excerpted from a publication issued by one utility.[30] According to this data, the cost situation at this coal-fired power plant (550 MW$_e$, 4,500 h/a) which started operating in 1985 is as follows: 0.013 DM/kWh for electricity generation; 0.013 DM/kWh for desulphurization; 0.008 DM/kWh for denitrification; 0.004 DM/kWh, each, for dedusting and other environmental-protection measures.

The calculation performed in table 12 for the entire SO_2/NO_x retrofit programme in the Federal Republic of Germany shows DM 0.015 for desulphurization and DM 0.01 for denitrification. However, since only half of the total electricity demand is produced in desulphurized and denitrified power plants, the impact on electricity price levels in the Federal Republic of Germany is likely to amount to only DM 0.013 on average.

Table 12

The additional energy generating costs of the total
SO_2/NO_x retrofit programme at power plants in the
Federal Republic of Germany

	SO_2	NO_x
Capital and other fixed costs	2.5	1.1
Energy	0.4	0.2
Reagents	0.1	0.1
Catalyst		0.1
Total annual cost (DM million/a)	3.0	1.5
Specific costs[a]		
DM/kWh	0.015	0.01
DM/kg emission abated	2.3	2.0

a/ Taking into account that, of the 360 TWh of electricity generated, approximately 200 TWh are produced in desulphurized power plants while around 150 TWh are produced in denitrified power plants with total emission reductions of about 1.3 million tons SO_2 and 0.7 million tonnes NO_x per year.

Figure 4
Breakdown of electricity generation costs for a 550 MW_e coal power plant
at a load factor of 4,500 hours per year

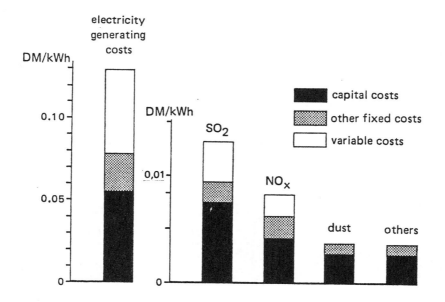

V. COST IMPACT OF SO2 ABATEMENT MEASURES IN THE NETHERLANDS

Consistent with the time horizon for policy analysis in the Netherlands, the analysis in that country focused on the years 2000 and 2010. An analysis of a 30 per cent reduction in SO_2 emission levels relative to 1980 was not undertaken because current policy in the Netherlands was expected to lead to reductions in the year 2000 in the order of 50 to 55 per cent compared to 1980 emission levels.

A. Underlying assumptions

The cost-impact analysis was based on certain assumptions[23] concerning base-case economic growth, energy demand, relative fuel prices, and diversification in the fuel-use capability of the electric power generation sector. The assumptions have been drawn from the intermediate economic scenario generated by the Central Planning Bureau of the Netherlands.

Table 1 presents assumptions regarding the development of key economic parameters and relative fuel prices during the period analysed. All prices are in 1985 Dutch guilders unless otherwise indicated.

Table 1

Key economic parameters and fuel price paths

	1985	2000	2010
World trade	100	180	267
GNP	100	156	195
Population	100	105	104
Dwellings	100	118	124
Personal autos	100	133	160
World crude oil price ($US 85/barrel)	26.00	30.00	35.50
Coal price (Dfl/ton)			
- Industrial users	197	192	211
- Electric power plants	169	179	196
Gas price (Dfl/m³)			
- Electric power plants	0.32	0.46	0.54
- Industrial users	0.43	0.46	0.54
- Households	0.56	0.65	0.75
Fuel oil price (Dfl/ton)			
- Industrial users	586	596	700
Petrol (Dfl/litre)	1.62	1.63	1.72
LPG (Dfl/litre)	0.66	0.67	0.74
Diesel (Dfl/litre)	1.00	1.02	1.13

Note: Based on these economic parameters and fuel price paths, the Central Planning Bureau of the Netherlands has calculated the expected final demand for energy by households, Government, industry and in the transportation sector in the years 2000 and 2010, taking into account energy conservation and shifts in the structure of industrial sectors consistent with the assumed economic development and fuel prices. Energy demand per sector is presented in table 2. These numbers include not only fuel and electricity demand, but also demand for feedstock.

Table 2

Energy demand by sector (PJ)

Sector	1985	2000	2010
Final Users:			
Households and Government	548	550	560
Industry	894	1 170	1 320
Other firms	345	320	360
Transport	326	370	430
Subtotal	2 113	2 410	2 670
Energy sector[a]	457	650[b]/620[c]	810[b]/710[c]
Total	2 570	3 060[b]/3 030[c]	2 990[b]/2 910[c]

a/ The energy sector includes electric power plants, refineries, and coke producers.

b/ Assuming 3,030 MWe of nuclear capacity and 6,290 MWe of coal-fired capacity in 2000; then 9,150 MWe of nuclear and 5,040 MWe of coal-fired capacity in 2010. Hereafter called the nuclear variant.

c/ Assuming 530 MWe of nuclear capacity and 9,290 MWe of coal-fired capacity in 2000; then 50 MWe of nuclear and 13,440 MWe of coal-fired capacity in 2010. Hereafter called the nuclear variant.

The final underlying assumption concerns the composition of public utility power generation capacity. Its composition has been calculated with regard to constraints on diversification in the fuel-use capability of the sector as a whole. Diversification is defined as the pursuit of generating capacity that allows for production of electricity according to certain prescribed fuel utilization. It does not, however, mean that actual power generation is constrained by a prescribed fuel-use pattern. Actual generation is determined by minimization of costs per kwh within the constraints imposed by capacity diversification. Table 3 presents the composition of the public utility sector power generation capacity.

Table 3

Public utility generating capacity, in MW_e

	1985	2000		2010	
		Nuclear variant	Coal variant	Nuclear variant	Coal variant
Nuclear	498	3 130	530	9 150	50
Coal	2 244	6 290	9 290	5 040	13 440
Gas	12 234	6 820	6 000	6 520	5 170
Wind turbines	0	720		2 000	
Public utility Co-generation	494	1 030		1 050	
Other	0	270		710	
Total	15 470	18 260	17 840	24 470	22 420

B. Emission reduction options

The SO$_2$ emission reduction options examined in the analysis include control technology options (flue gas desulphurization, fuel oil desulphurization, diesel fuel desulphurization, Claus tail units at refineries, and H$_2$S washing during the production of silicon-carbide) as well as fuel switching (greater utilization of natural gas by refineries and the electric power generation sector). The effect of (market-induced) energy conservation is taken into account in the projections of final energy demand (see table 2). Direct imports of electricity have not been considered in the analysis. Assumptions concerning the cost of control technology options are summarized below. All costs are presented in 1985 Dutch guilders unless otherwise indicated.

1. Flue gas desulphurization (FGD)

For a new 600 MW$_e$, coal-fired unit burning coal with a maximum 1.5 per cent sulphur content, with desulphurization of 100 per cent of the flue gas volume, producing gypsum as a by-product, the investment costs including all costs from both suppliers and owners, as well as waste-water treatment, have been calculated as Dfl 190 per KW, at a guaranteed SO$_2$ removal efficiency of 90 per cent.

Operating costs, including personnel, maintenance, waste disposal, inputs of raw materials and additional energy needs have been calculated based on 4,000 and 6,000 hours per year of operation at full capacity using fuel with an average sulphur content of 1 per cent. Annual capital costs have been calculated based on a 15-year write-off period and 8 per cent interest rate. Total costs are presented in table 4.

Table 4

Costs of FGD at a new 600 MW$_e$ coal-fired unit
(in Dutch cts per kwh, unless otherwise noted)

Investment (Dfl/kw)		190
Full load operating hours	4 000	6 000
Fixed operation and maintenance		
1. Operating labour and supervision	0.028	0.019
2. Maintenance	0.120	0.096
3. Plant and administration overhead	0.014	0.009
Subtotal	0.16	0.12
Variable operation and maintenance		
4. Raw materials	0.045	
5. Utilities	0.082	
6. Miscellaneous	0.013	
Subtotal	0.14	
7. By-product sales	None	
8. Cost of capital	0.55	0.37
9. Taxes and insurances	0.05	0.03
10. Interim replacements	Included under item 2	
11. Total costs	0.90	0.66
Total annual costs (Dfl million)	21.6	23.8
Total cost per ton SO$_2$ removed (Dfl)	1 270	930

Note: FGD investment costs for retrofit of existing installations are assumed to be approximately 30 per cent higher than FGD investment costs at new installations. FGD costs are also assumed to vary with capacity and installation size.

2. Fuel desulphurization

Heavy fuel oil

Reducing the sulphur content of heavy fuel oil from 1.5 per cent to 1.0 per cent costs approximately Dfl. 10 per ton heavy fuel oil, while a further reduction from 1.0 per cent to 0.5 per cent costs in the region of Dfl. 30 per ton heavy fuel oil.

Diesel fuel

Reducing the sulphur content of diesel fuel from 0.3 per cent to 0.2 per cent costs approximately Dfl. 15 per ton diesel fuel, while a further reduction from 0.2 to 0.1 per cent costs about Dfl. 20 per ton diesel fuel.

3. Process emissions

Claus tail units

Increasing the sulphur recovery of a Claus unit from 95 to 99 per cent will cost about Dfl. 750 per ton additional SO_2. It should be realized, however, that these costs are largely dependent on the unit capacity.

Sweetening (silicon carbide production)

The specific cost of lowering SO_2 emissions is approximately Dfl. 1,300 per ton SO_2 reduced.

C. Cost-effectiveness of control technology options

Given the costs presented above and estimates of uncontrolled emission levels consistent with the assumptions described in section A above, with respect to economic growth and energy demand, the various control technology options can be ranked according to their cost-effectiveness in reducing SO_2 emissions.

Emission reduction scenarios

The percentage of emission reduction is measured in relation to 1980 levels. A profile of this is presented in table 5.

Table 5

1980 SO_2 emissions in the Netherlands, by source category

Source	Kton SO_2
Electric power plants	195
Refineries	121
of which: combustion	(102)
process	(19)
Other industrial combustion	40
Non-refinery processes	51
Mobile sources	36
Other sources	22
Total	465

1. Current policy scenario

The current policy scenario examines the costs and expected emission reductions devolving from the SO_2 abatement policy currently being followed in the Netherlands. This policy involves regulations concerning fuel sulphur content and emission standards for various categories of installations. The main elements of the policy are summarized below.

New power plants and industrial installations for which a permit is granted under the Air Pollution Act after 29 May 1987 must meet the following emission standards:

- Coal-fired ......   > 300 MW_{th} 400 mg/m^3 + 85 per cent FGD
                                         < 300 MW_{th} 700 mg/m^3

- Oil-fired ....   > 300 MW_{th} 400 mg/m^3 + 85 per cent FGD
                                         < 300 MW_{th} 1700 mg/m^3 (corresponds to 1 per cent sulphur
                                                                 in the fuel)

- Refinery gas used outside refineries max. 35 mg/m^3

- Oxygas ....   max. 35 mg/m^3

- Coke oven gas .... max. 800 mg/m^3

- Blast furnace gas .... max. 200 mg/m^3

All existing coal- and oil-fired power plants for which a permit was granted before 29 May 1987 must meet the following standards as of 1 June 1987:

- Coal   > 300 MW_{th}, max. 0.8 per cent fuel sulphur content
                      < 300 MW_{th}, max. 0.8 per cent fuel sulphur content

- Oil   > 300 MW_{th}, 1700 mg/m^3
                      < 300 MW_{th}, 1700 mg/m^3

All existing coal- and oil-fired industrial installations for which a permit was granted before 29 May 1987 must meet the following standards:

- Coal   > 300 MW_{th}, max. 1.2 per cent fuel sulphur content (as of 1.11.87)
                      < 300 MW_{th}, max. 1.2 per cent fuel sulphur content (as of 1.11.87)

- Oil   > 300 MW_{th}, 1700 mg/m^3 (As of 1.6.87)
                      < 300 MW_{th}, 1700 mg/m^3 (As of 1.6.87)

Existing gas-fired power plants and industrial installations which were granted a permit before 29 May 1987 must meet the standards for new gas-fired plants as of 1 June 1988.

Existing coal-fired power plants and industrial installations which were granted a permit to burn coal in a new unit before 29 May 1987, and which will still be in operation after 31 December 1994, and existing coal-fired power plants and industrial installations for which a revised permit to burn coal in a modified unit was granted before 29 May 1987 and which will still be in operation after 31 December 1999, must meet the following standards as of 1 December 1989;

> 300 MW_{th},   400 mg/m^3 + 85 per cent FGD

< 300 MW_{th},   max. 0.8 per cent fuel sulphur content (power plants)
                        max. 1.2 per cent fuel sulphur content (industrial installations)

Existing oil-fired power plants and industrial installations which were granted a permit before 29 May 1987 and which will still be in operation after 31 December 1994 must meet the following standards as of 1 December 1989:

> 300 MW_{th},   400 mg/m^3 + 85 per cent FGD
< 300 MW_{th},   1700 mg/m^3

Refineries

Combustion emissions from refineries may not exceed 2,500 mg/m^3 during the period 1 January 1986 through 31 December 1990. The total of combustion emissions plus process emissions may not exceed 2,000 mg/m^3 during the period 1 January 1991 through 31 December 1995. The total of combustion emissions plus process emissions may not exceed 1,500 mg/m^3 for the period beginning 1 January 1996. Refineries are to comply with these emission standards largely through the greater utilization of natural gas.

Diesel fuel

The maximum allowed sulphur content in diesel fuel was 0.3 per cent. This has been reduced to 0.2 per cent in the Netherlands before 1 January 1989.

2. Target level scenario

The current provisional environmental quality objective of the Netherlands with respect to acidification, as announced in the Indicative Multi-Year Programme for Air 1985-1989, is geared toward the prevention of acidification's most serious detrimental effects. This provisional quality objective of 1,400 acid equivalents per hectare per year is currently being re-assessed and the possibility of revision cannot be excluded. However, for the purpose of this analysis, the SO$_2$ emission reduction necessary to achieve this objective has been postulated as scenario 3 in accordance with the outline prepared by the ECE Group of Economic Experts on Air Pollution.

In order to achieve the provisional environmental quality objective, SO$_2$ emission reductions to the order of 70 per cent relative to 1980 levels are needed in the Netherlands (simultaneously with reductions in the order of 30 per cent for NO$_x$

and 50 per cent for NH^3 in the Netherlands as well as 70 per cent for SO$_2$ and 30 per cent for NO$_x$ overall in Europe). The Netherlands has no policy in place for achieving a reduction of this magnitude.

Various measures are technically feasible although other considerations, such as economic, financial, political or organizational factors, could preclude their implementation. The costs and expected emission reductions associated with several technically feasible possibilities are presented in this document although their inclusion does not imply that they would be judged optimal, or even acceptable, if all policy criteria were taken into account.

The technical possibilities analysed include:

(a) Further flue-gas desulphurization (to 95 per cent) at electric power plants, assuming the same average sulphur content in coal as that currently prevailing, namely 1.27 per cent. The same emission reduction could, however, be attained through utilization of coal with a lower sulphur content or through a combination of lower sulphur coal combustion plus flue-gas desulphurization;

(b) Further replacement of heavy fuel oil by natural gas at refineries;

(c) Further fuel-oil desulphurization by industrial users, namely from 0.2 to 0.1 per cent sulphur for middle distillates and from 1.0 to 0.5 per cent for heavy fuel oil.

3. Costs and expected emission reductions of the scenarios

Table 6 presents an overview of the costs and remaining SO$_2$ emissions of the scenarios described above.

Table 6

SO$_2$ emissions and annual abatement costs by scenario, in 2000 and 2010

Year 2000, source	Scenario 1	Scenario 2
Electric power plants	76/53*	27/20*
Refineries	71	20
of which: combustion	(62)	(11)
process	(9)	(9)
Other industrial combustion	29/32*	18/21*
Non-refinery processes	26	26
Mobile sources	26	26
Households and Government	5	5
Other	7	7
Total emissions (Kton)	240/220*	128/123*
Abatement costs (mln. 85 Dfl/year)	583/474*	857/716*
Year 2010, source		
Electric power plants	100/33*	35/13*
Refineries	75	22
of which: combustion	(65)	(12)
process	(10)	(10)
Other industrial combustion	40/45*	28/33*
Non-refinery processes	30	30
Mobile sources	28	28
Households and Government	3	3
Other	8	8
Total emissions (Kton)	284/222*	155/138*
Abatement costs (mln. 85 Dfl/year)	755/425*	1070/654*

* Coal variant/Nuclear variant

VI. COST IMPACT OF SO2 ABATEMENT MEASURES IN POLAND

The activities of Poland to decrease SO_2 emissions from internal sources include administrative and technological measures. With regard to administrative measures, in 1980 a reduction to half the existing standard of admissible SO_2 content in air for 1990 was declared in order to put administrative pressure on air polluters. As for technological measures, the main thrust of direct abatement efforts is a programme for a 50 per cent reduction of the 1980 SO_2 emission level from the 1980 emission sources by the year 1995. This would result in a 30 per cent reduction of the 1980 SO_2 emission level (or even slightly more) by the year 2000, even taking into account new SO_2 emission sources created with power generation developments after 1980.

The programme is a cumulative effort of coal mining, power generation, metal and chemical industries. It has been based on some general assumptions taken as valid for 1985: no significant changes of fuel mix except the addition of nuclear power plants and no significant new imports of primary energy have been envisaged. Therefore, the existing fuel mix used for power generation (predominately hard coal and lignite) will limit possibilities of fuel substitution. Consequently, the main stress is on improvement of fuel quality and abatement techniques.

Table 7

Investment and operational costs for 30 per cent reduction of 1980 SO_2 emissions in Poland by the year 2000

Investment	New plants investment cost	Retrofit plants investment cost	Annualized operational costs
		(Millions of 1985 US dollars)	
Fuel desulphurization			
Coal wet cleaning (S > 1.5 per cent)	283		73
Coal wet cleaning (S < 1.5 per cent)		453	149
Oil desulphurization		415	62 *
Flue gas desulphurization			
Wet limestone scrubbing	692		104 *
Limestone addition		126	19 *
Combustion modernization			
Fluidized bed combustion	220		35 *
Other approaches		377	---
Process emissions removal		629	94 *
Total	1 195	2 000	536

*Denotes estimate

VII. EXPENDITURE ON AIR POLLUTION CONTROL IN THE UNION OF SOVIET SOCIALIST REPUBLICS

Under the Tenth Five-year Plan, capital investments for air pollution control[29] amounted to 837 million roubles. This sum represents under 0.4 per cent of total capital investment in industry. In 1981 capital investment for air pollution control was 141 million roubles and in 1982 it was 145 million roubles. The relationship between capital investment and pollutant removed is presented in table 13.

Table 13

Investment and reduction of air pollution in USSR for the years 1975-1982 (in millions of roubles)

	1975-80 (yearly average)	1981	1982
Investment	167	141	145
Reduction of air pollutants (in millions of tons)	2	1.3	0.7
Kilogram of pollutant removed per rouble	12	9	5

VIII. EXPENDITURE ON AIR POLLUTION CONTROL IN THE UNITED KINGDOM

There are no statistics available on total expenditure in the United Kingdom for air pollution control. The following individual items form an important part of the programme.

A. Power stations

The Central Electricity Generating Board (CEGB) (and National Power/PowerGen, after privatization) will spend over £1 billion on: retrofitting three power stations with flue-gas desulphurization (FGD) equipment; fitting 12 stations with low-NO$_x$ burners; and equipping new stations with both FGD and low-NO$_x$ burners. CEGB recently announced the award of the first £300 million contract to retrofit Drax. The overall total and timing will depend on decisions to be taken by the companies in consultation with, for example, the Government's pollution inspectorate.

B. Large combustion plants

Substantial further expenditure is anticipated for compliance with the new Directive of the European Communities (EC) adopted in November 1988, requiring 60 per cent reductions in sulphur emissions from large power stations and other major plants from the 1980 levels by 2003, and 30 per cent reductions in nitrogen oxide emissions from the 1980 levels by 1998.

Vehicle emissions

The "Luxembourg package" of measures adopted by the EC in December 1987, and further measures agreed in November 1988, will lead to substantial reductions in NO$_x$, CO and hydrocarbon emissions from motor vehicles. United Kingdom motoring costs are expected to rise by £850 million per year after full implementation of the new standards.

REFERENCES

1/ The macro-economic impact of environmental expenditure, OECD, Paris 1985, pp. 25-26.

2/ The macro-economic impacts of the EEC large combustion plants directive proposal, Institute for Environmental Studies, Amsterdam 1987, pp. vii-viii.

3/ Umweltschutz und Wirtschaftswachstum, Forschungsberichte 2/86, Bundesministerum für Gesundheit und Umweltschutz, (in German) Vienna 1986, p.16.

4/ H. Alfsen, D.A. Hansen, and L. Lorentsen, Tax on SO_2 emissions from fuel combustion: Policy analysis on a Norwegian general equilibrium growth model, 1987, p.9.

5/ Cf. reference 2, p. viii.

6/ S. Khodorkovskaia, "The effectiveness of protection of the atmosphere", in: Problems of Economics, Vol. XXVII, No. 11, March 1985, New York, pp. 61. Also available in Russian "Effektivnost okhrany vozdushnogo basseina", Voprosy ekonomiki, Pravda, 1984, No. 6, pp. 89-97.

7/ Cf. reference 4, p.15.

8/ International Conference, Environmental and Economics Background Papers, Vol. 1, OECD, Paris 1984, p. 243.

9/ K. Aiginger, Politische Thesen zur Versöhnung von ikonomie und ikologie, in: Wirtschaftspolitische Blätter 4/1986, Vienna 1986, p. 454.

10/ Preliminary assessment of costs and benefits of reducing emissions from large firing installations in the Federal Republic of Germany, EB.AIR/GE.2/R.13, 1985, p.10.

11/ IFO-Institut für Wirtschaftsforschung, Beschäftigungseffekte der Umweltpolitik, (in German) Munich, 1979.

12/ Beirat für Wirtschafts-und Sozialfragen, (in German) Umweltpolitik, Wien, 1986, p. 79.

13/ Cf. reference 6, p.61

14/ Cf. reference 2, p. vii.

15/ Cf.10 reference , p.10.

16/ T. Johannsen, "Strategies for reducing sulphur and nitrogen emissions in relation to energy production structure and energy use", in: Technologies for Control of Air Pollution from stationary sources, Economic Bulletin for Europe, Vol.39, No. 1, 1987.

17/ The macro-economic impact of environmental expenditure, OECD, Paris 1985, p.86.

18/ Macro-economic consequences of a policy to save energy and to abate acid rain emissions in the Netherlands, paper prepared by A. Nentjes and G. Klaassen for the symposium "Acid Rain and the European Economy", Utrecht, 1985, p.9.

19/ Cf. reference 3, p.12.

20/ H.H. Härtel, K. Matthies and M. Mously: Zusammenhang zwischen Strukturwandel und Umwelt, (in German) Hamburg, 1987, p. 224.

21/ Cf. reference 3, p.18.

22/ Cf. reference 20, p.200.

23/ B.H. Tangena, (RIVM) Optimalisatie bestrijding verzurende emissies, 's-Gravenhage, February 1985 (Dutch edition); Nationale Energie Verkenningen, 1987, Energie Studie Centrum, Petten, September 1987 (Dutch edition).

24/ Aufwendungen der Industrie für den Umweltschutz 1982-1990, Bundeskammer der gewerblichen Wirtschaft, (in German) Vienna 1987.

25/ Cf. reference 3, p.90.

26/ The Sulphur Commission Report I, Ministry of the Environment, Finland 1985.

27/ Données économiques de l'environnement, Ministère de l'Environnement, (in French), Paris, 1987.

28/ J. Jung, Investitionsaufwand für die SO_2 - and NO_x-Minderung in der deutschen Elektrizitätswirtschaft, in: VGB Kraftwerkstechnik, Heft 2, (in German) February 1988.

29/ B. Schärer, N. Haug and H.J. Oels, Costs of Retrofitting Denitrification, in: Federal Environmental Agency (Ed.). A Selection of Recent Publications (Vol. 2), Berlin (West) 1988.

30/ Badenwerk, Umweltfreundliche Kohleverstromung, Fachberichte 88/1 (in German).

31/ Cf. reference 6, pp.59-73.